Inside Hollywood

Inside Hollywood

Poetry, Lyrics, Art and Erotica

By

Marsha Ross

ISBN-13: 9781983754128
ISBN-10: 1983754129

About the Author

MARSHA ROSS, the author of INSIDE HOLLYWOOD, is an artist and writer, who ran away from a traumatic, toxic family, in Colorado, at the age of seventeen, with less than a thousand dollars. At the age of twenty-two, with less than two thousand dollars, she traveled around the world alone.

She has spent much of her life travelling, gathering inspiration, and trying to do good. She received her BA in Psychology, Cum Laude and her MFA in film writing and production, both from UCLA.

She lives in Laurel Canyon in Los Angeles, hidden in the woods with a dog, a cat, and a mountain in her backyard. Her art has been exhibited around the world, including New York, Paris, Los Angeles. Tokyo and New Delhi. Her work offers the viewer scathing insights into various subjects including Political satire, drug abuse, sexuality, spirituality, the Hollywood system, feminism, nature, and Rock'n Roll. Her art decorated NICKY BLAIR'S famous celebrity restaurant on Sunset Strip for over ten years.

She created PHOTOSPHERE, Los Angeles' first photographic art gallery, also on Sunset. It made national news three times and Elton John came to the grand opening. It featured exhibitions of Edward Weston, Laser Photography, Album Cover Art, and Erotica, among others.

While still in film school, she wrote the famous NEW YORK MAGAZINE cover story HOLLYWOOD FIGHTS BACK, and was the magazine's Hollywood Correspondent to the Cannes Film Festival. She wrote the LOS ANGELES MAGAZINE cover story 'WHY HANDSOME DOESN'T MAKE IT ANYMORE, and other magazine articles. She got to meet the powerful and famous Hollywood filmmakers, lawyers and artists. She has written screenplays and did album cover art for billboards, album covers and ads in BILLBOARD and CASHBOX. She worked at the United Artists Art department and

Warner Brothers Film Studios. She created the famous Marv Gaye billboard on Sunset Strip, for his last album on "WHAT'S GOING ON?" Capturing a unique moment in history; it featured her photograph of a line of solarized purple police in riot gear, who were marching on the students at UCLA, on the day that they shut down the campus, trapping the then California governor, Ronald Reagan, in the faculty lounge that enraged the students that the United States invaded Laos.

She worked with the world hunger project, where she created and imagined THE WORLD THE WAY IT IS, a sociological dramatic game experience, designed to reveal and understand why hunger exists even though there is no scarcity of food in world. It was televised twice at the LA Convention Center, by three hundred Hollywood power players.

She worked as a professional photographer and journalist to support herself and to pay for her nine years at UCLA, earning her MFA from the UCLA film school and both her Bachelor's and Master's degrees in Psychology. She worked uncovering malingering in psychiatric credibility testing, and studies genetics. She has written comedy screen plays, made funny and beautiful short films, which are featured on the Marsha Ross Channel on YouTube. She traveled around the world alone when she was 22, and again at the age of 28. In London, long before 9/11, she was introduced to a handsome young Saudi Prince, the son of the late governor of Mecca. He enrolled in the Georgetown School Graduate School of International Relations, without even filling out an application.

They became great friends and lived in a mansion outside of Washington D.C., on Chainbridge Road, right on by the Potomac River in Arlington, Virginia, along with his handsome young entourage, including his closest friends, a French chef, drivers, servants, and bodyguards.

She attended his classes, read his books, taught him about nuclear threats, and wrote his assigned 20 page final thesis paper about America's intervention in Grenada. Marsha claimed the intervention was a staged event, to change the news from the hundreds of American soldiers killed in Beirut, two days earlier. It was later published in book about American interventionism, which pleased his royal family.

He went back to Saudi Arabia, after just one semester to great reviews. In an elevator in the Nairobi, she met the foreign minister of the new country, eventually became Los Angeles Permanent Diplomatic Counsel for the POLISARIO Guerilla Front.

The refugee camps were run by the Saharaoui women, while the men fought the guerilla war and were returning from the guerilla war. Both the men and the women often wore blue jeans and t-shirts. They slept during the day, and they worked and played at night. She worked at the UN and lobbied Washington to stop providing Morocco two million dollars a day worth of leftover napalm, to exterminate the native Saharaoui people, who hid under their tents and died. She helped stop the aggressors who wanted to annex the Sahara to steal the mineral rights, which included the world's second largest deposits of phosphates as well as uranium, gold, and silver. She felt she had to help stop this genocide.

She traveled to Algiers, and the refugee camps in the Sahara desert, and met with the CIA, and the State department, to enlist their help. The CIA rewarded her with an operative in her post-graduate theater directing class with Lee Strasberg, shortly before his death. James Baker was finally called upon to stop America from helping Morocco kill the beautiful, nomadic Bedouin Saharaoui people. Now the country, known as the Western Sahara, exists, and is on every atlas, globe, and map of the world.

MARSHA ROSS GALLERIES, features her own unusual, expressive art, Indian and Tibetan religious art, and her large collection of the art of Milton Glaser, the famous New York artist who created the "I love NY" campaign. Marsha's art is also available also her website, SPIRITUALSURREALART.COM. And Marsha is peaceful, happy, and INSIDE HOLLYWOOD, again.

Inside Hollywood

In Passing

Like the prince of darkness
you came with the night.
At ungodly hours
an irresistible sight creating
unearthly worlds for me
to play in
to wonder and delay in
always serious
extraordinary delight.

Taking me beyond strangeness
to times and places
mystical spaces
nothing can erase.

Magical gardens
overgrown with dreams
come alive for my amusement
then disappearing
without a trace.

A slave girl
a concubine
a mistress
a creature that could soar

All of this you promised
you delivered even more.
And when the games were finished

when the imagining was through
in the midst
of all the darkness
I fell in love with you.

Now yours completely
choosing freely to obey
with nothing left to conquer
you tried a different way.

You became a lover
infinitely tender
and took away my pain

traded it for promises
rainbows and tomorrows
days that never came.

For you went back
to darkness
and I went in search
of light.

I wanted you in sunshine
though we only touched
at night.

Of course you knew better
having played this game before
that with the daylight
comes the truth
and the truth is
you're a whore.

I wish I never ripped
the mask
from off your face
mystery once uncovered
cannot be replaced.

And that which thrives in darkness
It will die without a fight
like a lie exposed to truth
It will shrivel
in the light.

But still, I remember loving
and who would have guessed
that the game you played
in passing
was the game you played the best.

Bright Eyes

Bright eyes
who misses
nothing
we were here to visit.

Smiles blond
and curls of red
bounced upon your trampoline
and ate your sunshine.

We laughed in your corners
and rippled in your air
I smiled underwater
and floated in a chair.

We sailed amidst your treetops
tasted your tangerines
tiptoed through your tulips
and acted in your scenes.

We slid along
your surface
and ran naked
through your mind

as you probably noticed
my friend
she ate a peach
and I more formally dined.

Nonsense and Delusion

Hollywood is full of nonsense,
delusion and egomania.
They think that plastic surgeons
will keep them
young and beautiful forever
though they aren't even young
or beautiful now.

Magic

Magic and garbage
lost and found love
collecting
washed-up dreams
like seashells
on the beach

❧

In Hollywood

Everybody's got a script to sell or
someone else they want to be

✧

Life in the Movie Business

Life in the movie business
is like life itself…
full of surprises
and constantly yelling,
I've been screwed.

❧

In Darkness

I wait
in darkness
for your smile.
It says so much,
suggests such grand conspiracy.

Great Agents

The key to being a great agent
is to treat a celebrity
like a normal person
and everyone else
like a celebrity.

⁂

Prime

In between
the madness
and the bed sheets
lie the moguls
and the beggars
dwells the midnight mystery
hauntingly transparent
even in my solitude.

She's an artist.
She don't look back.
Yet there she is
giving life
to lifeless forms by night
and playing so many
games by day.
crying out silently,
Why does no one penetrate
the prime of my life?

Bathroom Water

Hollywood is like Dali's bathroom

❧

Beyond

Somewhere
far back
beyond freedom
beyond dignity
or even equality

beyond logic
or necessity
even beyond choice
rational or otherwise

beyond thought and
even emotion
somewhere beyond,
beyond but always now
I am yours.

Swirling

Swirling
whirling
spinning
choices

upset the pieces
on the board
change the odds
in a moment

teach new rules
that make no sense.
Die, lose
steal success
with a winning hand

we can create magic
in the middle of a life
and with a little luck
we can cheat tomorrow.

❧

Success

The recipe for Success
in Hollywood
is nepotism
and money

sex or family
usually some
or more likely
all of the above.

An Animal Caged

Night creeps in like a cat burglar
finds me thrashing
like an animal
caged by its own
caress
awaiting yours to set me free.

The Hollywood Cage

Hollywood has always been a cage…
a cage to catch our dreams.

For Your Soul

Hollywood is a place
where they will pay thousands
for a kiss
and fifty cents for your soul.

Crazy

In Hollywood
if you don't have a shrink
people think you're crazy.

❧

No Sanctuary

Fame is no place
for the passing of youth
suicide is much easier
and more acceptable in Hollywood
than growing old ungracefully.

Sea of Stars

Soft
black velvet
stretched in a sea
of stars
yawns.

The Mad Queen

The mad queen
was here to visit.
she came in flowing red
and lace.

she brought her book,
her flag and her pillows
to get some freckles
on her face.

Garbage and Limousines

Garbage and limousines
toothless monsters
next to billboards of toothpaste models

smiling emptiness
winners, losers.
There is nothing
worse than to be lost
in between.

My Soul

My soul
left vulnerable
would run away
but there is nowhere to go
I am the beast.

Love Lost

Empires decline
wars leave rubble
love lost
only leaves
love lost.

❧

Wounds

Leftover gestures
made to past lovers
indignify the present
and make the past
laughable.

Wounds not quite healed over
send me dodging
invisible
nonexistent pain.

Crying out
to the silent voids
of unspoken promises,
made in Hollywood
and never kept

Meeting You

Years ago
I opened a door
and took your hand.

I had never seen you
or God
before

yet I had to force
my fingers
to let go.

I had known you
long before
that first touch

and always
loved you
at first sight.

I tasted God
electricity in your kisses
magic.

We were one
even before
we were lovers

with our bodies
that fit together
so perfectly.

Even in our separateness
nothing came between us

Three thousand miles away
you held me through the night.

Limitless passion was our
creation electromagnetic
expression, bliss and
completion.

Never again
would we be alone
or curse the gods
at last
we were in love.
Out of our minds
tasting only infinity.

Yet even we
who knew the ways
of deities and kings

chose the path
of mortals
sacrificing love to the ordinary
and mundane.

For you were inexperienced
in matters of the heart
and I was still a child
who tried to hold
a rainbow

instead of hide it
from the light.

A little smarter now I
would be grateful just
to see your colors.

Associate Producer

An Associate Producer often is
the only one in Hollywood
who will associate
or sleep
with a producer.

The Tide Pool

Tide pool of
swirling images
quixotic
quicksand
of imagination
pulls me back
to dreams once lived
to lives once dreamed
erasing the differences
before my weary eyes

An Early Death

Now I see
through the gateway
of senseless pain
lies a place

that is empty
where life
goes on
without thought

in arenas
without audiences
in ballrooms
without partners

where the past
dances with the future
street-corner vendors
sell the truth

win or lose
pay the same
and love always dies
an easy death.

Einstein

Einstein says,
"Nothing can be lost,
it can only change forms"
so where does lost love go?

Busy Lover

Making love
somehow becomes
out of the question
there are so many things to do.

Designing cookie boxes
cooking tomato soup
teaching morons
how to think.

Anything now
is preferable
to intimacy
the humiliation
of innocent parties

is the only issue
you claim
avoiding yourself
is really the game.

Package it
design it
make it sterile
wash it clean.

Perhaps in time
even I who loved you most
will forget your touch
if not your name.

❦

Magic and Garbage

Magic and garbage
Lost and found love
Collecting
washed up dreams
like sea shells
on the beach.

❧

Rolls Royce Elegance

Wealthy Samurai
Dancing among the peasants

Rolls-Royce elegance
making it all yours.

Terrifying little white girls
with tales of love and slavery
brandishing your sword
and lighting up the night.

Exciting Samurai
Vanishes with the morning
Leaves behind almost conquered
willing inspired delight.

Secretly I surrender
warrior of the night

and gently plead with fate
for a swift return of you
and your sweet pain.

The Cosmos

The cosmos
is a varied
expression
of light
the essence
of consciousness

Mind is
the channel
to consciousness—
really the only
suitable vehicle
to explore the cosmos.

Having Thought Myself Complete

Having
become the source
waited in outer
corridors of the universe
until I accepted knowledge
as the way.

Found the truth
and thought myself
complete
if once again
I could touch you
I would know nothing.

❧

Light Beam

What do you suppose
it might be like
to sit on a light beam
and travel with it
throughout the night?

Potholes

Swirling purple potholes
of sucking sadness
pull me in
to windowless
gray corridors

of faceless faces
and past reminiscences
slightly too pink
and gay.

Between My Sheets

Lions and tigers
between my sheets
disappear
when the light comes on.

Alone

The quiet death
I attended alone
part of me
and you
torn from my body
in a moment of sanity
with irrational consent
along with my loneliness
alone.

New York City

New York City
where one-night stands
don't come easy
and survival
is on everybody's mind.

New York City
forgot its manners
saves its smiles
for regular customers.

Stone and steel hearts
pinnacles of civilization
flowers growing
between the concrete.

When you're hungry
even cynicism
tastes sweet
in New York City.

Obey

In Hollywood if you
obey all the rules,
you miss all the fun.

Prostitutes and Sissies

Hollywood makes prostitutes
out of women
and sissies out of men.

Lock Me Up

Lock me up
chain the body
let the mind
wander.

Allow unfettered existences
bound by nothing
not even gravity.

In fact, forget gravity
Lock it up
and make me laugh.

Life is an instant
the space between two breaths.
Stop breathing

stop time
stop the universe
stop laughing.
There's nowhere else to go.

Discrimination

Hollywood is the definition of sexual discrimination.

❧

In Between

In between
the madness
and the bed sheets
lie the moguls

and the beggars
dwells the midnight mystery
hauntingly transparent
even in my solitude

she's an artist
she don't look back
yet there she is
giving life

to lifeless forms
by night
and playing so many games
by day

crying out silently
why does no one
penetrate
the prime of my life?

I Wait in Darkness

I wait
in darkness
for your smile.
It says so much
suggests such grand conspiracy.

⥈

The Game

Just think of it
as a bad roll
in the Monopoly game

go directly to jail
do not pass go
do not collect $200

lose the next two turns
and pay $250 for your
abortion . . .

don't matter 'bout
Boardwalk and Park Place
when the game of life
got you beat.

The Telephone Rings

Dear and distant lover
you will call me Monday morning
and the phone will ring
and ring and ring.

What will you think?
Do not despair.
I have not forsaken
our ritualistic electronic connection

traversing time and space
for the arms of another.
Nor have I broken my link
with radical chic.

Do I ignore your ring?
No, it is quite a different thing.
Simpler than that
and much more profound.

The telephone rings
but makes not a sound.
It has been disconnected
for Nonpayment.

Who Can Blame You

Poor
unenlightened child
product of Western civilization
who meditates on a light bulb
and thinks God is something packaged
with Mom and apple pie.
Who can blame you
for dreaming your life
away?

❧

It's Okay to Cry

Open your eyes,
look at me,
fix your attention
on something

said the ugly nurse
through the pain
as the invisible doctor
behind the white curtain

of my thighs
sucked
mercifully
away

the baby
that couldn't be born.
"Open your eyes," she said.
"It's okay to cry."

Contact

Thank God
for the phone company
and my gynecologist
keeping my lines clean.

my only contact
with the outside world
I let the doctor
touch me

and the phone man
ring my bell.
as I play it safe
in a fertile universe.

California and the Judge

She loved easily
saw good
in little things
especially funny men.

He made her laugh
and before she could see
his robes of black
she was in love.

He judged one and all
who came before him.
Even the ones he met
undercover

in his blue jeans
and cowboy boots.
He found them all lacking
somehow unworthy

most likely guilty.
Used to crime and lies
He did not look for
or easily find virtue.

He pounded the gravel
on a deserted beach
at a roadside coffee shop
in her bed
while she loved him.

And he found her guilty.
Like all the rest
not quite perfect
and not to be blessed.

But the verdict
delivered as an afterthought
was shattering
nonetheless.

Killing newborn dreams
leaving little time for appeal
before the jailer locked
her heart up

and taught her once again
not to trust.
And that God
has his own plan.

Hollywood Christmas

Hollywood Christmas
blinking neon
red and green

cannot mask
abandoned child
Christmas blues

Holiday delight
smile on us all
and say a prayer

for some of us
who can't say one
ourselves.

Especially wish goodwill
and painless dreams
to those of us

who sleep alone
in Tinsel Town
tonight.

Love is Everywhere

Energies
centering
on the uncontrollable
surrendering
to the moment.

Knowing
that love is
everywhere.
Not just here
or there.

❧

Sad Song

Melancholy haunts my mind.
Your sad song Lingers,
Drifting among my thoughts
Settling nowhere.

My Love

My love for you
is as timeless
and mysterious
as the great Sahara

forever changing always
the same forbidding
and dangerous strange

unconquerable
and rich
textured and varied
with potential energy

incalculable
until released
like water rushing to the sea
to meet itself.

I seek the truth
and wait for you
to take me home
with you.

Little Orphan

Here comes the little orphan
like Annie and her dog
unprotected, open, vulnerable
at once and always powerful
grown-up child of the mind

Covering the pain she feels
in just the nick of time
searching in the night
for a why or wherefore
to make it all seem right.

Daddy Warbucks
has eluded her
and there is no hope in sight.
Here comes the little orphan
and with her comes the light.

❧

If You Would Only Sing

I'd be a dancer
if you choreographed
a cashier
in your café.

Cook short order
in your diner, sweetheart
serve pork and beans
at your buffet

roll out your red carpet
if you were a king
I'd be your microphone, baby
if you would only sing.

❧

Truth

I came to dance
to surrender
to the universal truth
to float

in the channel
of creativity
that some
call truth

And others know
to be simply
more elaborate
illusion

I'll Play it Cool

If my honesty doesn't please you
and you find
games more intriguing
just say the word

Of course I'll play.
I'll deceive you
and hide from you
and cheat in different ways

I'll play it cool
some dirty pool
and lie right to your face.
I'll satisfy

your sick desires
ruin our love so free
Too bad a greater passion
was not in your heart for me

Dreamer

Dreamer
The sexual revolution
is over.

Wake up!
Life always kills
The dreamers.

And the world would
certainly not be so colorful
without you

Certainly
we lived a dream
revolting even against our very own reality

lost in magic
passion and sexuality.
But it's over.

The revolution is over
it's been co-opted and compromised
and the dangers
have become too great

So it's time to
wake up. Please,
loved one before
it's too late
awaken.

Real life
always kills
the dreamers.

❧

Have Mercy, Jailer

Have mercy, jailer
When will the memories
fade?

So that sleep disappears
And I don't dream
that you're awaiting at the door

waking both of us
still crazy with passion
our love still intact.

When will you
disappear
from my thoughts
and fantasies?

When will you unlock
my heart
and uncage
my mind?

You Punish Me

I begged
you promised
no more lies
let truth
be all
between us.

But honesty
is a silly thing
and now demands
you punish me
with silence.

You disappear
your body stays
it is some sort
of violence.

You no longer
say I love you
instead you punish me
with silence.

My Apologies

So good-bye
young love
and my apologies
for life is not ideal

Even the chosen
must suffer indignities
but dishonesty
destroys us

and love
gets lost
in silence
It is some sort of
violence.

More or Less

Dangerous man
I will not run away.
You scare me
but I will not hide

nor will I fight.
I can do
no more or less
than honorably surrender
to my fate.

Your Face

Now the faceless man
in and of my dreams
has a face
Your face

※

Easy

How easy
you make it
to shut the door
on yesterday

❧

Before your Touch

Before your touch
enslaved me
I did not wait.

Now I am
an artist made docile.
A woman.

So like all women
now I wait.
A prisoner of war.

In solitary confinement
awaiting your touch
to set me free.

I Come Freely

I come freely
will follow
willingly
and obey joyfully
For I have waited
forever
for you

Late Again

Oh My
you're late
which I hate
and I'm getting tired

more so
by the minute.
What do you think
of matinées?

I Will not Cry

I do not mind
that I love you
more
than you will ever
love me.

For I have more love
to give
and to feel it
is an incredible joy

And I will not cry
because you squandered
your love on those
who came before me

For I am but a beggar
at your table
and a feast from any other
equals not your crumbs

So do not stand
on ceremony
or principle
weighing

that
which can't be measured
with the idea
to set me free.

Just please let me
continue to love you
more than
you love me.

❧

The Fairy

If a fairy
now appeared
and granted me a wish

it would not be
for fame or wealth
beauty or happiness
or even perfect health.

Loved one
I'm embarrassed
to admit

but strangely compelled
nevertheless
to tell what is true

and that is certainly
that I would beg the fairy
only to spend
my life with you.

Power Over Me

I give you too much power
over me
With a kind word
you make rainy days disappear

or with an
undeserved reproof
you darken
the brightest hour

You can turn
if so disposed
away any gray cloud
that visits me

as surely as
your retreat into
your well-worn shell
will turn my sunshine blue

❧

Eternity

We take nothing away
of this world
when we die
and die we must

So to accumulate anything
but ecstatic moments
of perfect being and completion
seems sheer foolishness to me

Dearest one
do not strive
for false idols
or more wealth than you need

goals which will
leave you cold
when life is gone
or if you're lucky even sooner.

Love will keep you warm
if you dare to let it
until the very last moment
if not long past eternity

Switzerland

California winters
are never severe
sunshine in January
it rains twice a year.

And Switzerland
in winter is covered with snow
freezing cold
twenty below.

A nightlife, A bright life
glamorous LA
where producers produce
and players play.

Conservative and quiet
workaday Swiss
I'd trade all the high life
I used to call my life
to be part of this.

To be quiet
and peaceful,
safe and
serene
normal and protected

healthy and clean.
From this smog-laden city
with its drugs and its crime
it seems like a dream.

Loving You

Why does
Loving you
feel different
dangerously
complete
painfully delicious
soulfully nutritious
sinfully sweet?

Can't Fool the Wise Man

I told
The wise man
I had loved
too passionately

Lived the life
of a fool
for more
than a few years

In fact,
For a relatively long time.
Indeed remarkable
said the wise man

So many moments lost
But then I never really
knew him that I loved
so passionately said the fool

Of course not
revealed the wise man
that is why
you were able to love him

And now
empty and serene
and peaceful
but somehow mysterious

lonely nights
find me wishing
I was still
the fool

Why

Why?
after it's all over
when all the pain
and the explaining are through

just when I thought
indifference had set in
when it no longer
mattered

who was wrong
or who said what
or did what
to whom

or even how many times
you broke my heart.
Why is it that after all
none of it matters anymore.

Why when it's all supposed
to be over
do I find myself
still in love with you?

❧

Safe Harbor

From the unknown
mysterious desert
comes silent ageless strength
to calm the storm-tossed night

Forbidden love
Tastes that much sweeter
Awakened innocence
too long buried

beneath endless layers
of cynical sophistication
emerges
toward the light

Feelings surface effortlessly
in your waters
yet like all true men
of the sea

you pull in your anchor
and head for the unknown
leaving me cast adrift
by convention

and diving even deeper
in search for that
elusive safe harbor
I once found in you

Fugitive

Long after
the thought
the love and pain
were gone

your face
in a crowd
sent me chasing
my escaped fugitive

dangerously threatened
heart before it terrorized
further self-destructing
before my weary eyes.

I Beg You

As you well know the
moment is you.
So it is no wonder
that no matter how hard I try

it is impossible to pretend
that I do not love you. I
have heard it said that
passion will conquer all

even fear itself
but that time waits for no one.
So putting pride aside
I beg you to love me. Now
Artist

Artist

Good-bye, dear love
and try to understand
I'm an American
I grew up in Disneyland

with Mickey Mouse
and fairy tales
magic kingdoms
and dreams that came true

when you wish
upon a star
or become one
where adventure and reward

still await the brave
who take the risks
and dare
the unknown

And I still
believe in happy
endings, love in
truth
and fair play

the power of trust
and transcendent imagination
More than a mere American
I'm a child of Hollywood

I make fantasy
become reality
as a matter of routine
and celluloid histories

more permanent than anything real.
True, I lack a certain cynicism
I'm embarrassingly naive
romantic—even innocent

in spite of myself
a true believer
to the very end
so I'm sure you understand

how one
such as I
could be such a fool
as to believe in you

꧁꧂

Lover

Friend protector
inspiration
wonderful artist

words could never express
all you are
and always
have been to me

encouragement
when I'm blue
always my best friend
understanding

even my worst loneliness
a teacher
banishing
ignorance

most of all
giving me
the special gift.
Of extended youth

Dearest One

Dearest One
I will never
be able to express

my gratitude
for my life
for my ability to love

for my mind
all of which
you so gently expanded

The Oldest Wolf
In the Forest

The oldest wolf
in the forest
knows all the tricks

How to trap the innocent
and seduce
the unaware

The weak stand no chance
against his practiced cunning
his graceful approach

and his innocent smile
masking dangerous teeth
and intentions

as he lures
yet another unsuspecting creature
into his lair

and moves in for the kill.
Do not make
the same mistake

Years have not gentled him
only refined
the traps he sets

New blood
and fresh souls
are what he seeks

The oldest wolf in the forest
is not even hungry
expert that he is

it takes little effort to feed him
and weakness is
all around

But still, he hunts
and kills now
simply for the thrill
and to remember how it feels
to be young again

❦

THE END

White Goddess

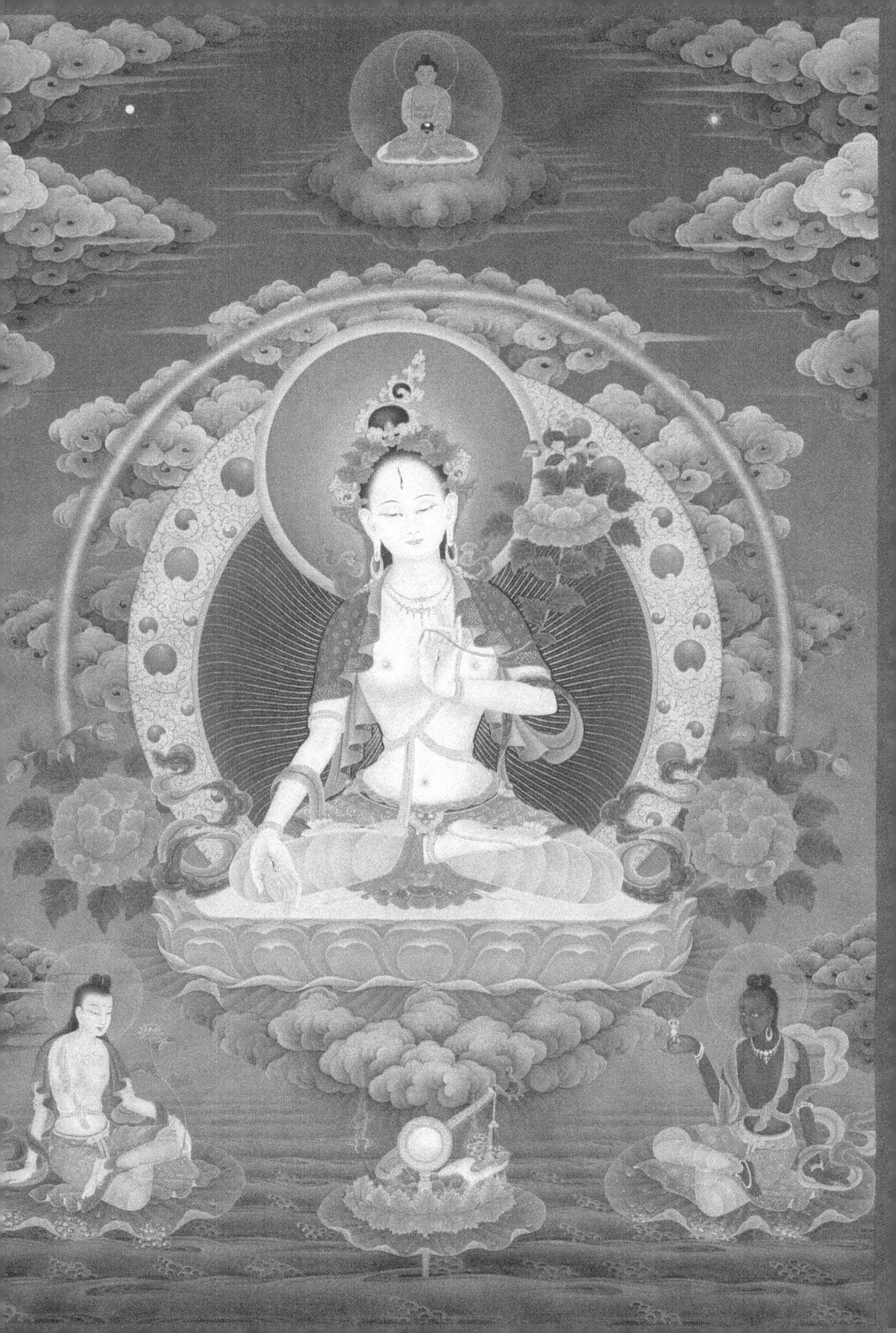

ancient starfish

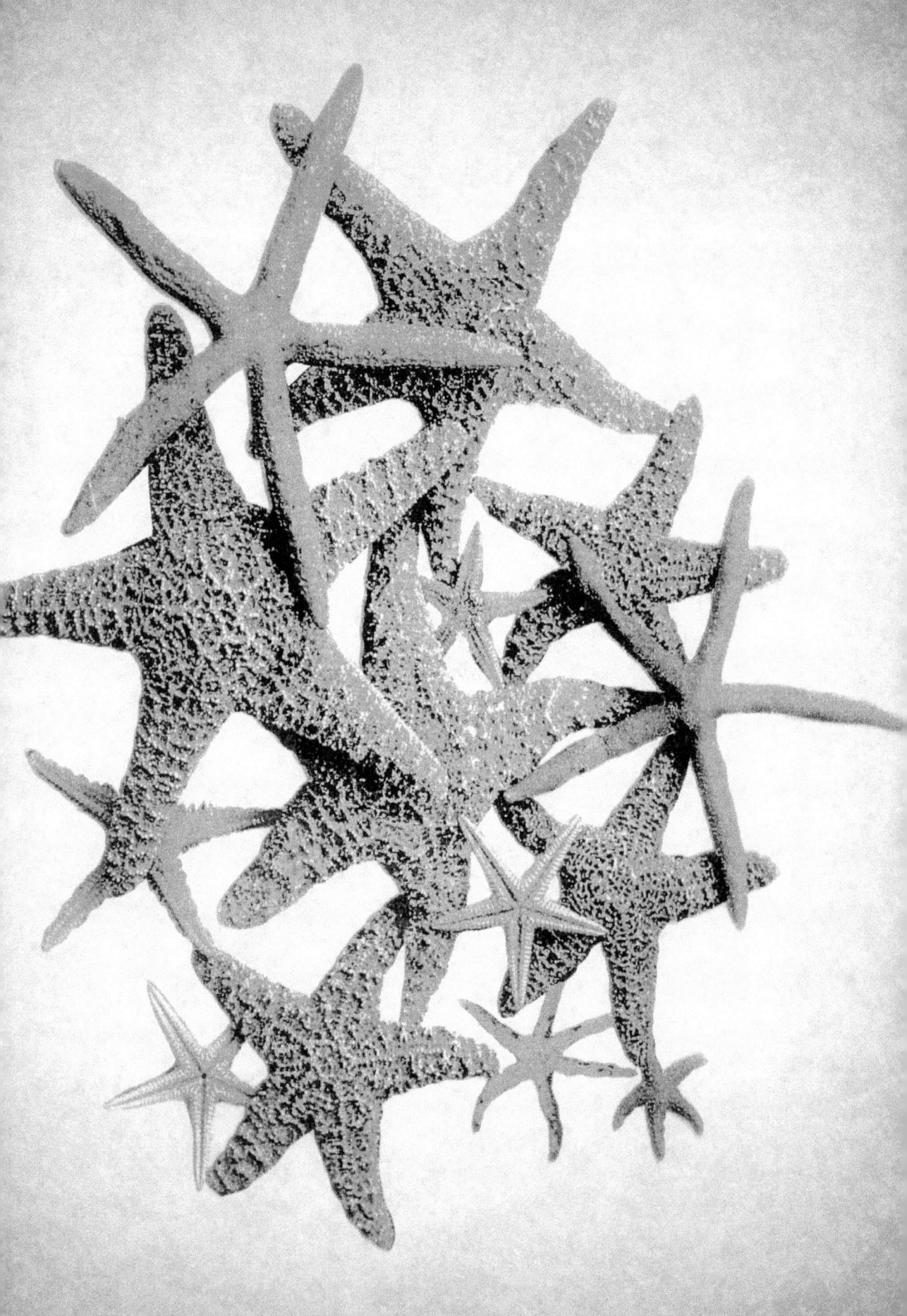

animal nature

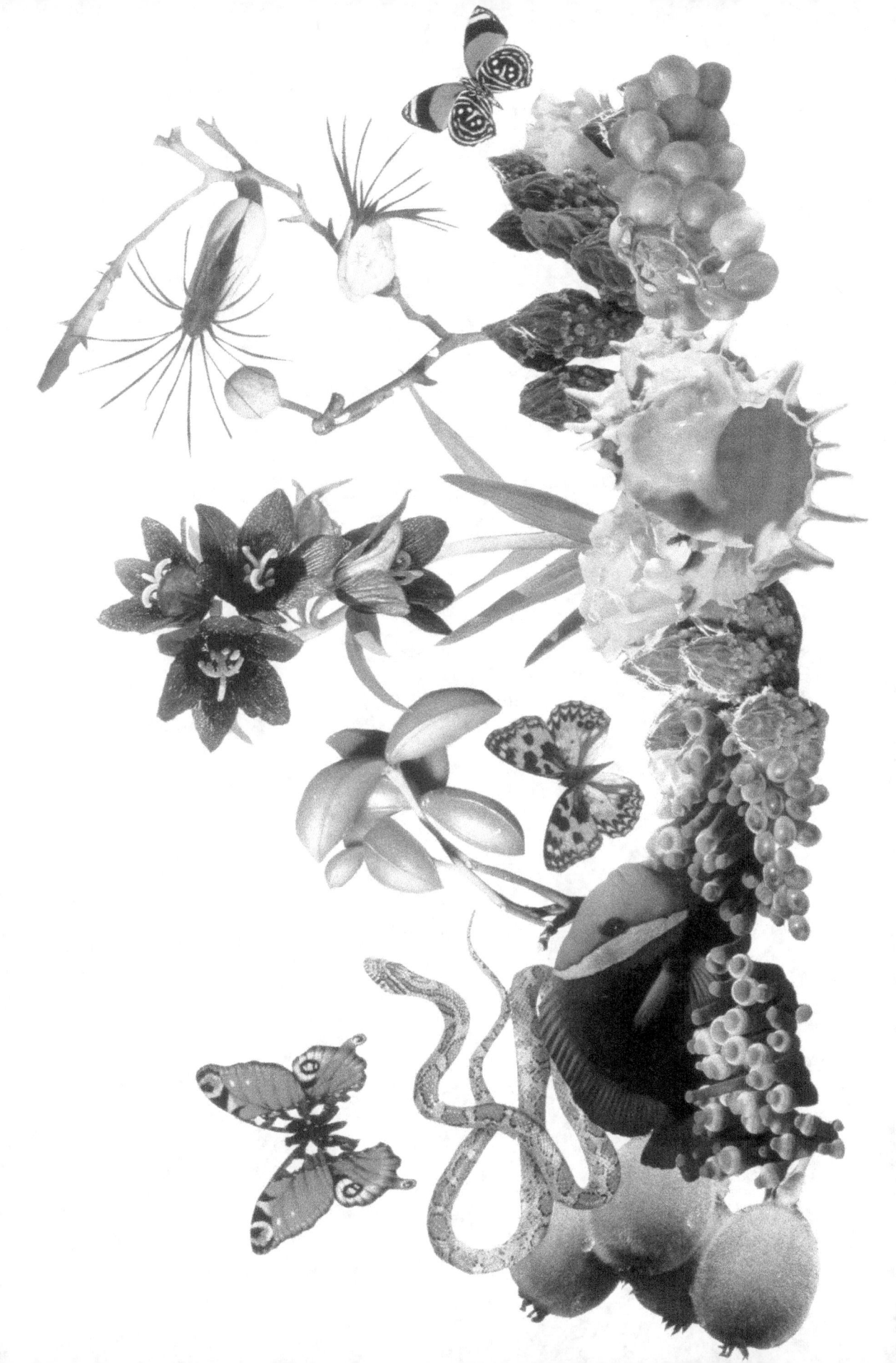

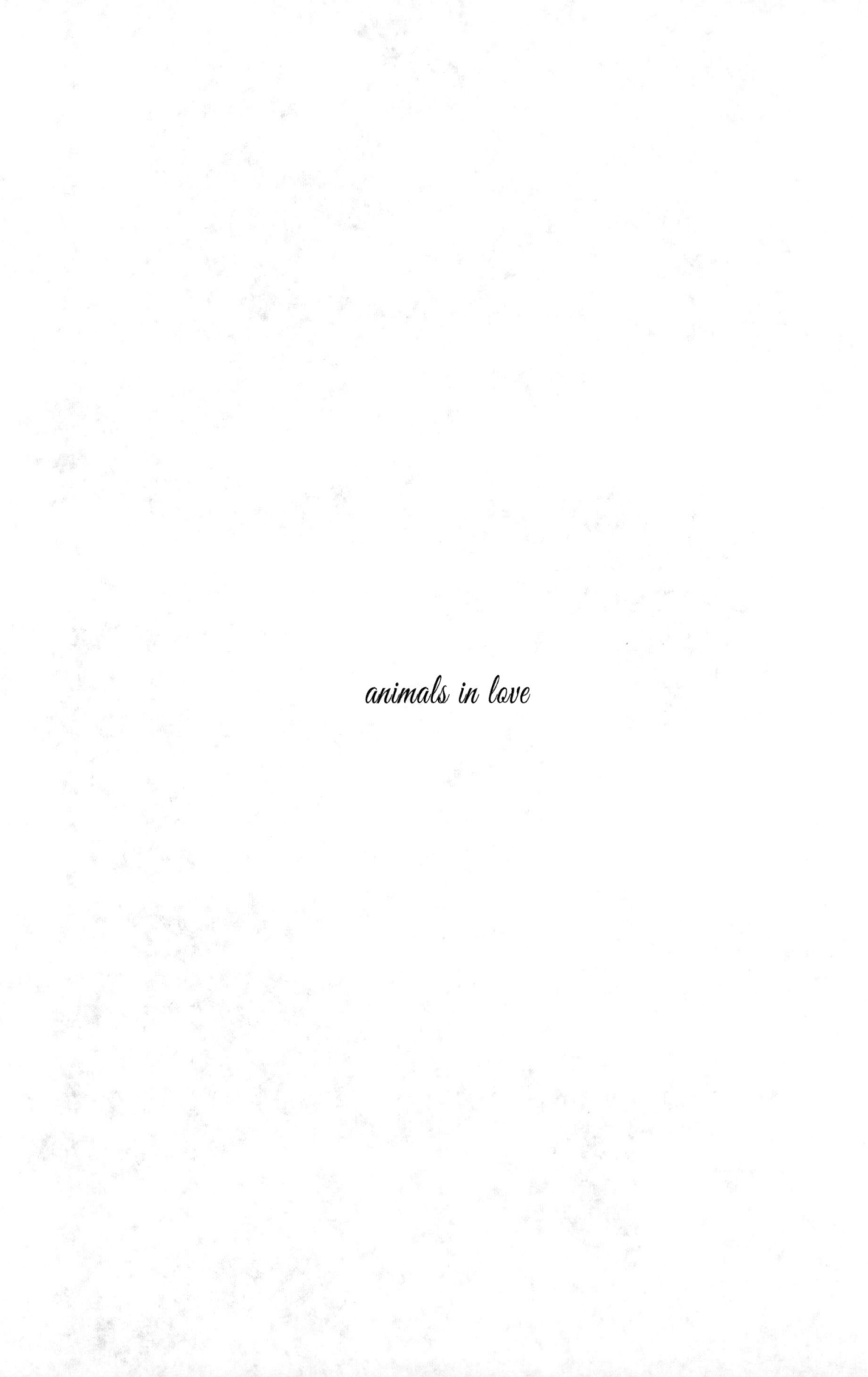

animals in love

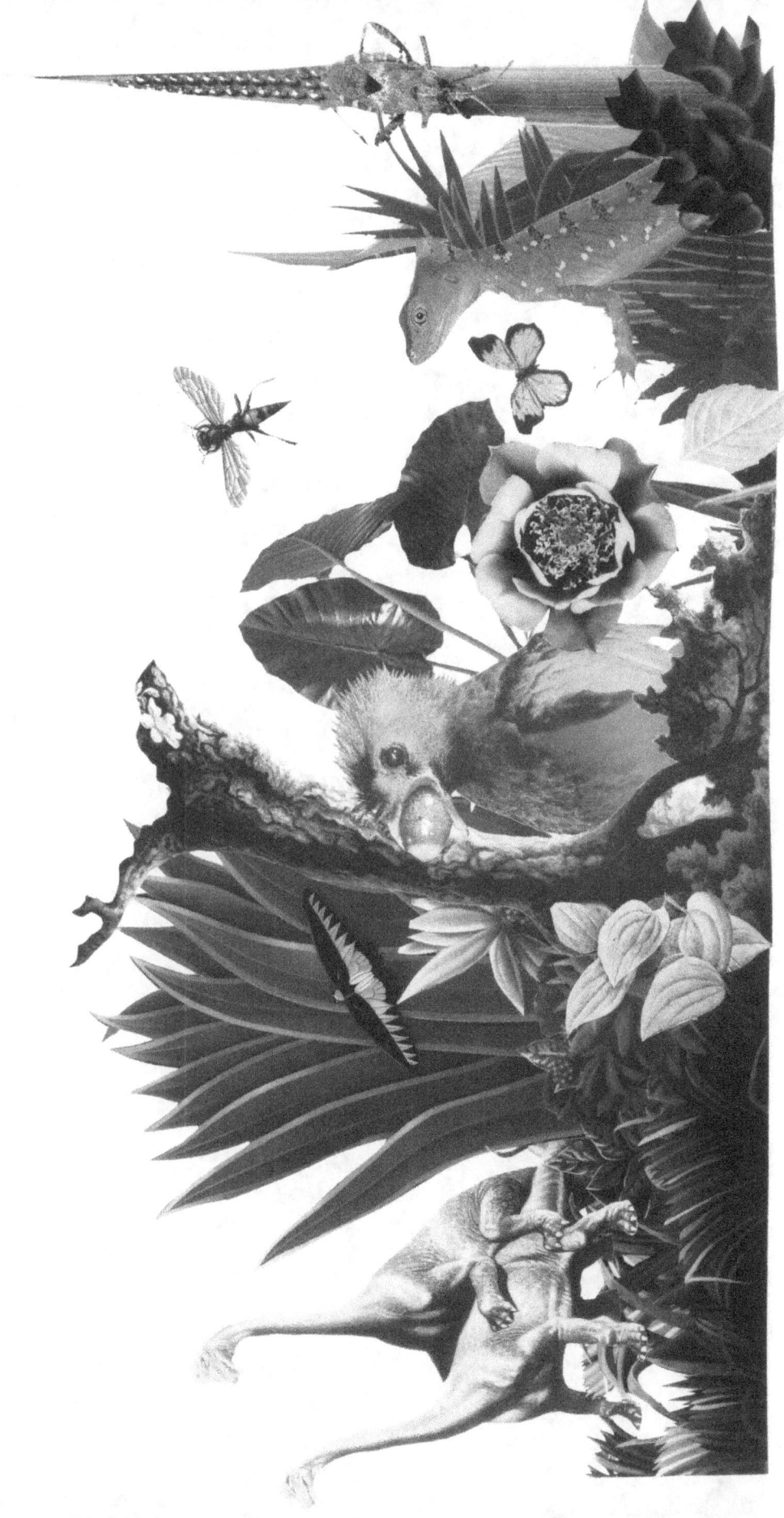

Aquarium

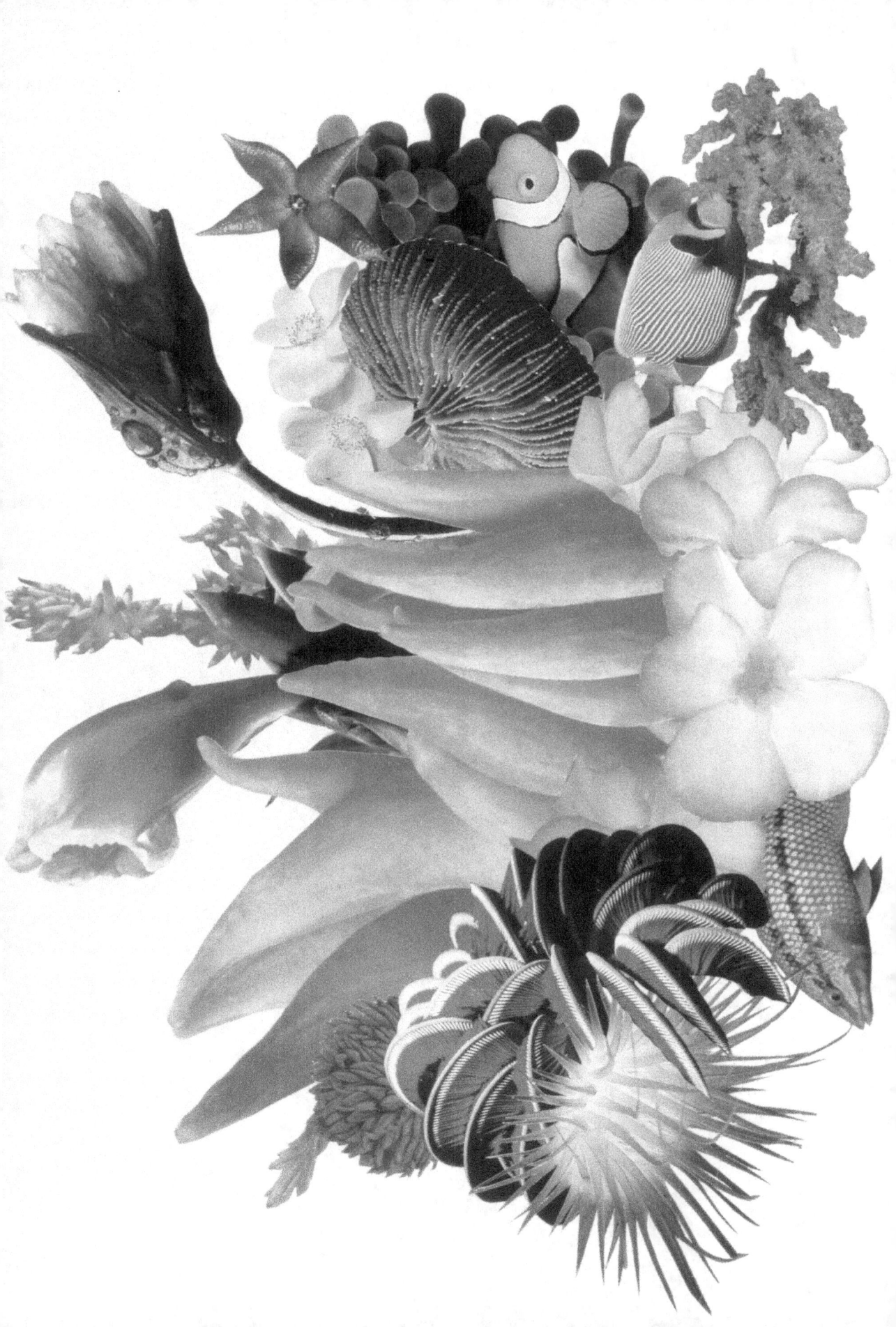

butterflies

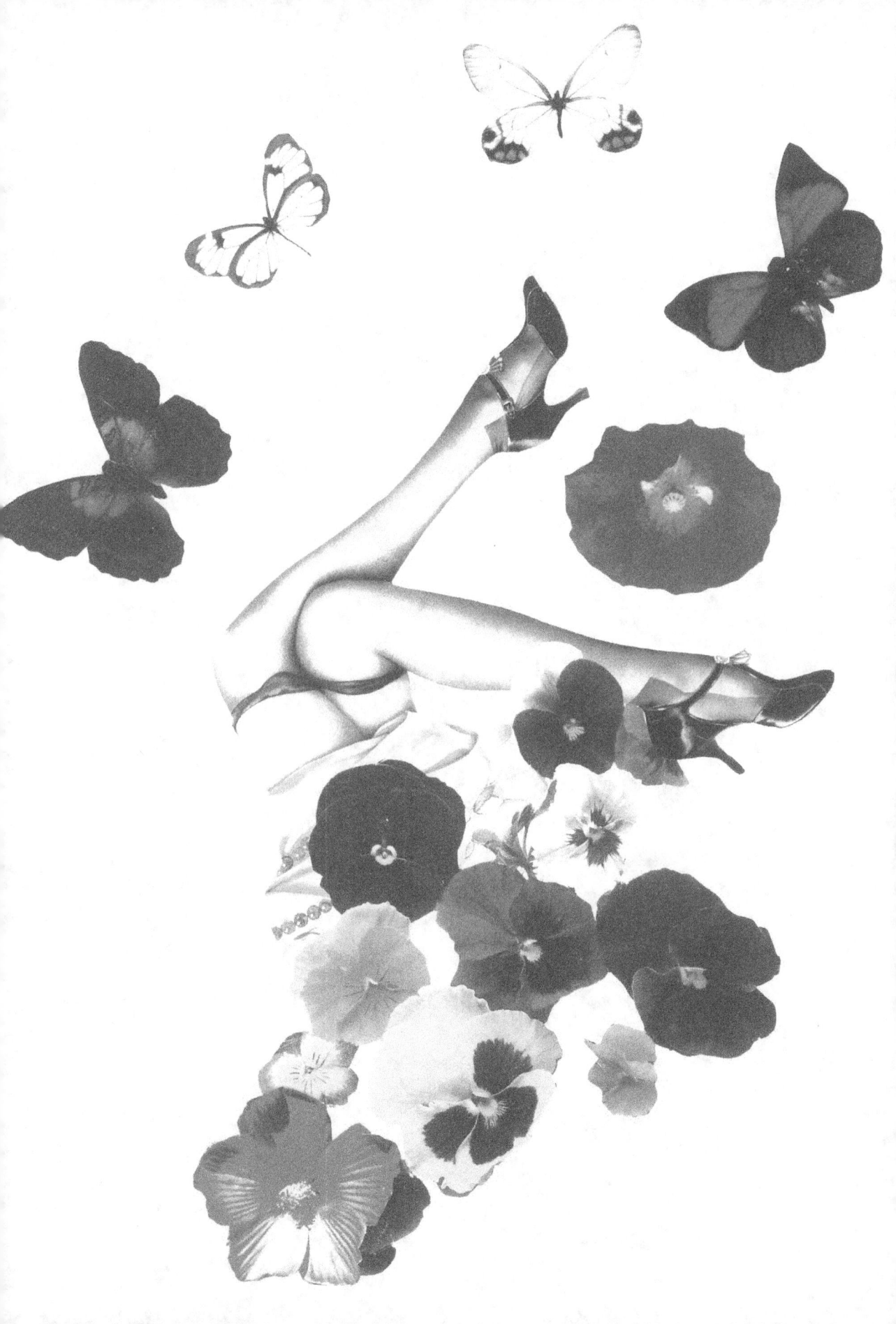

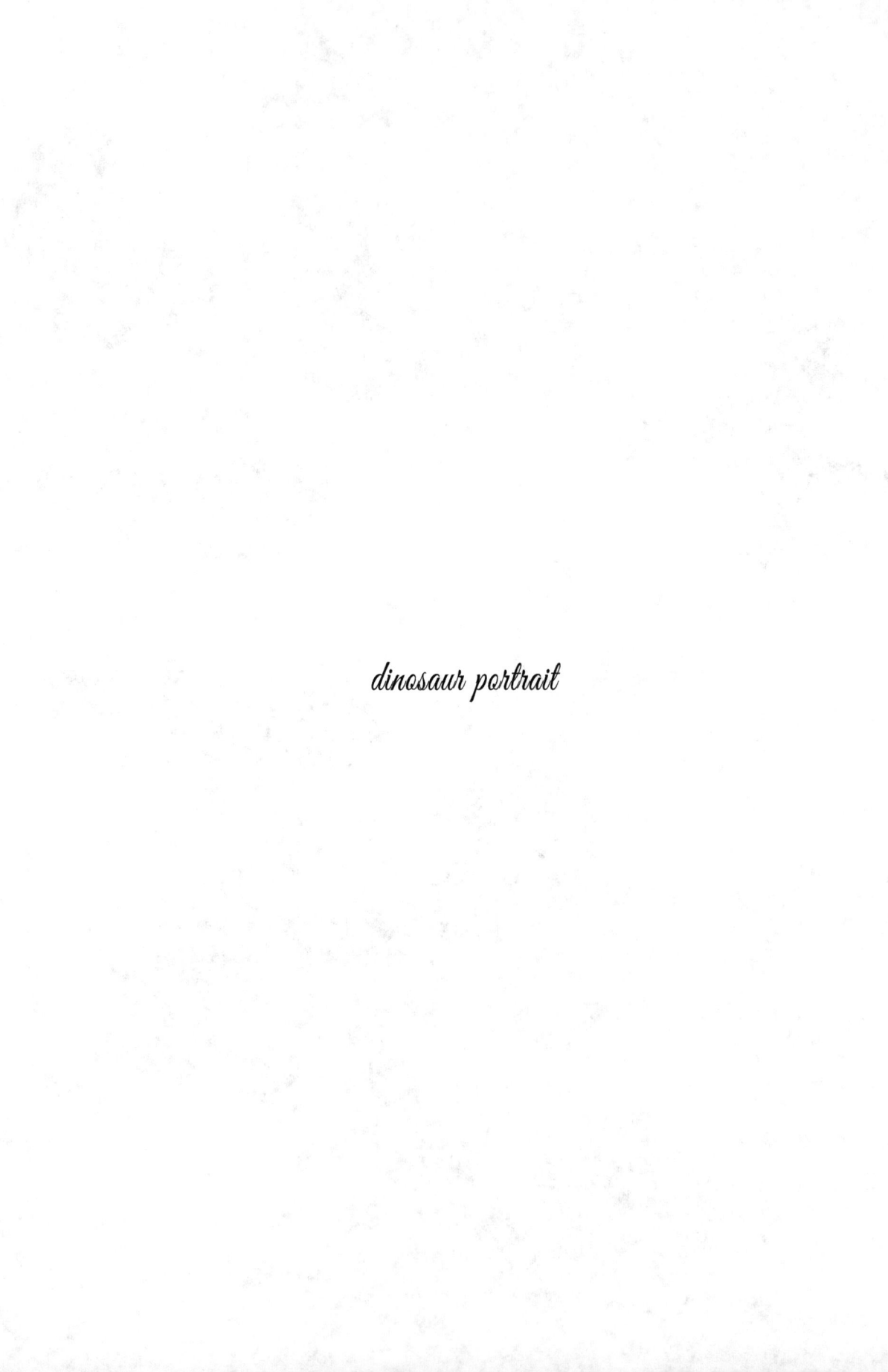

dinosaur portrait

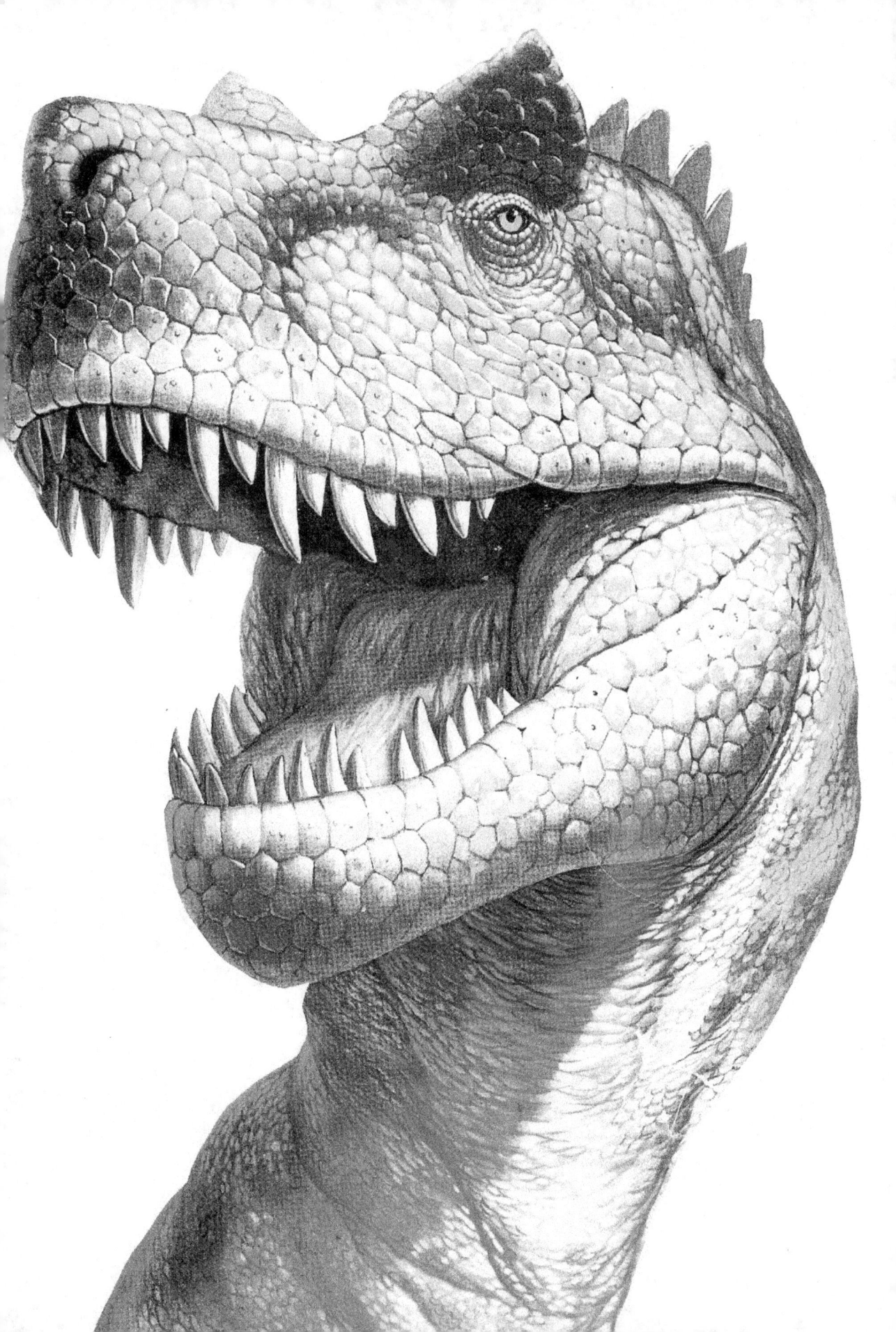

Dragon Goddess

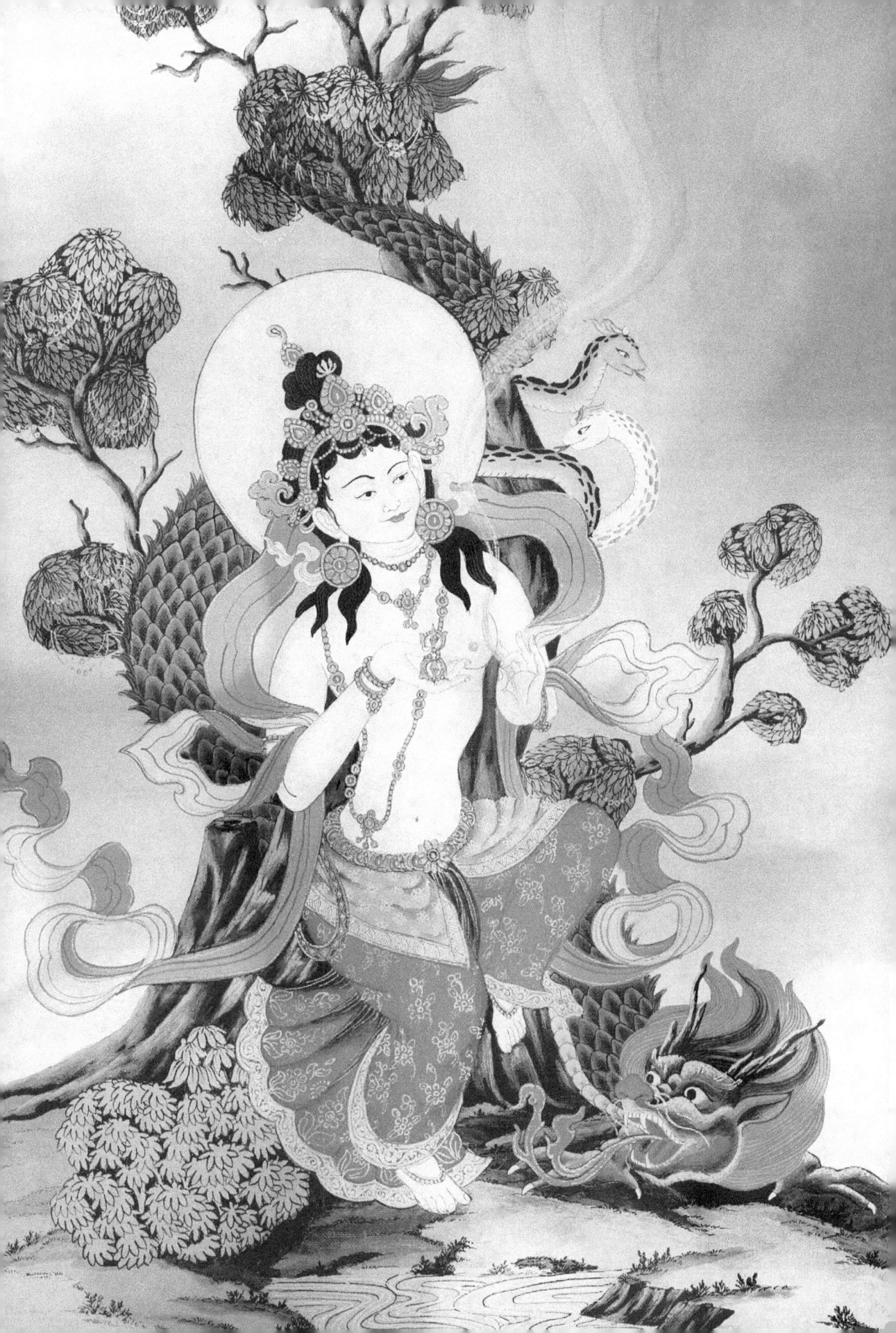

favorite frogs

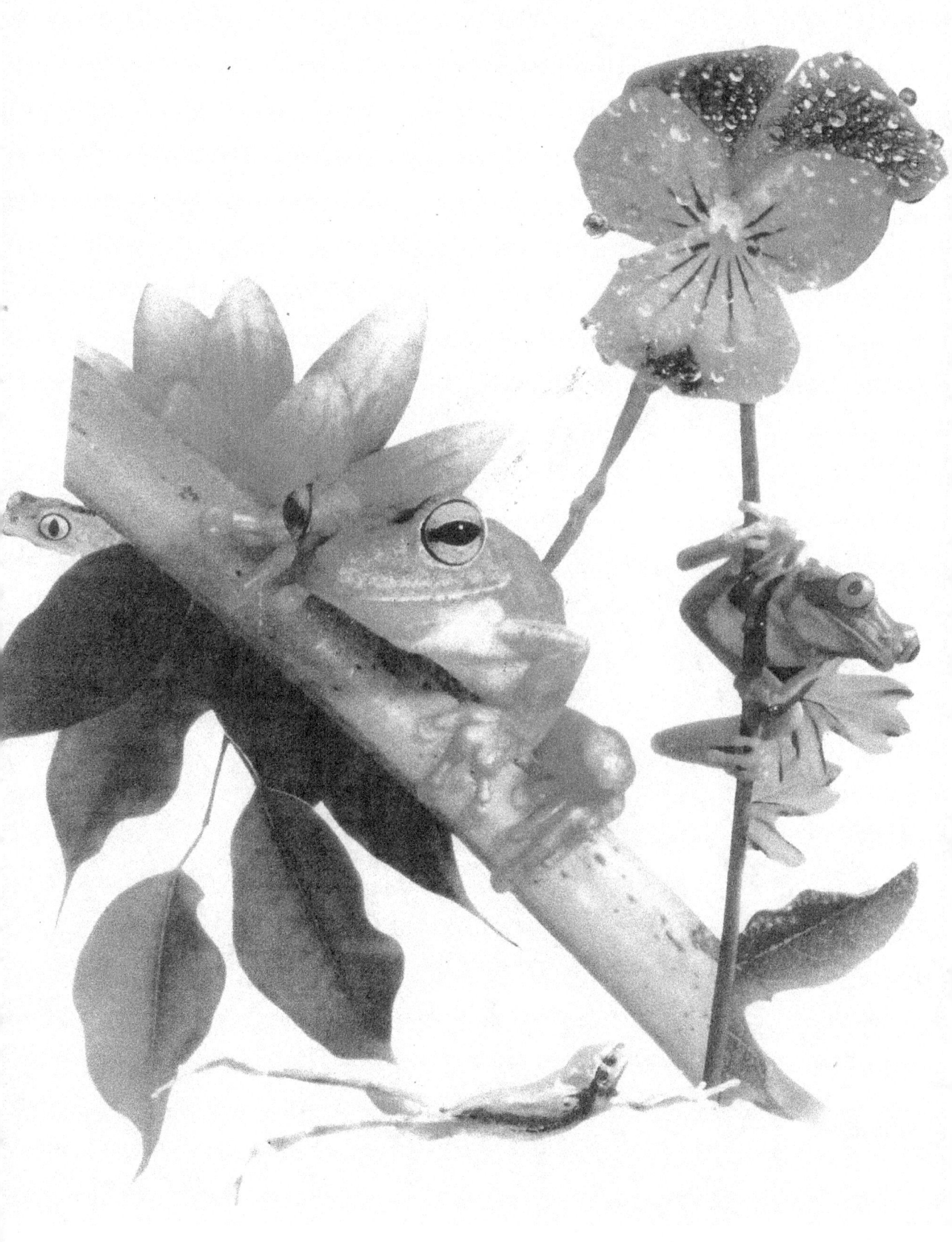

Flower Shop

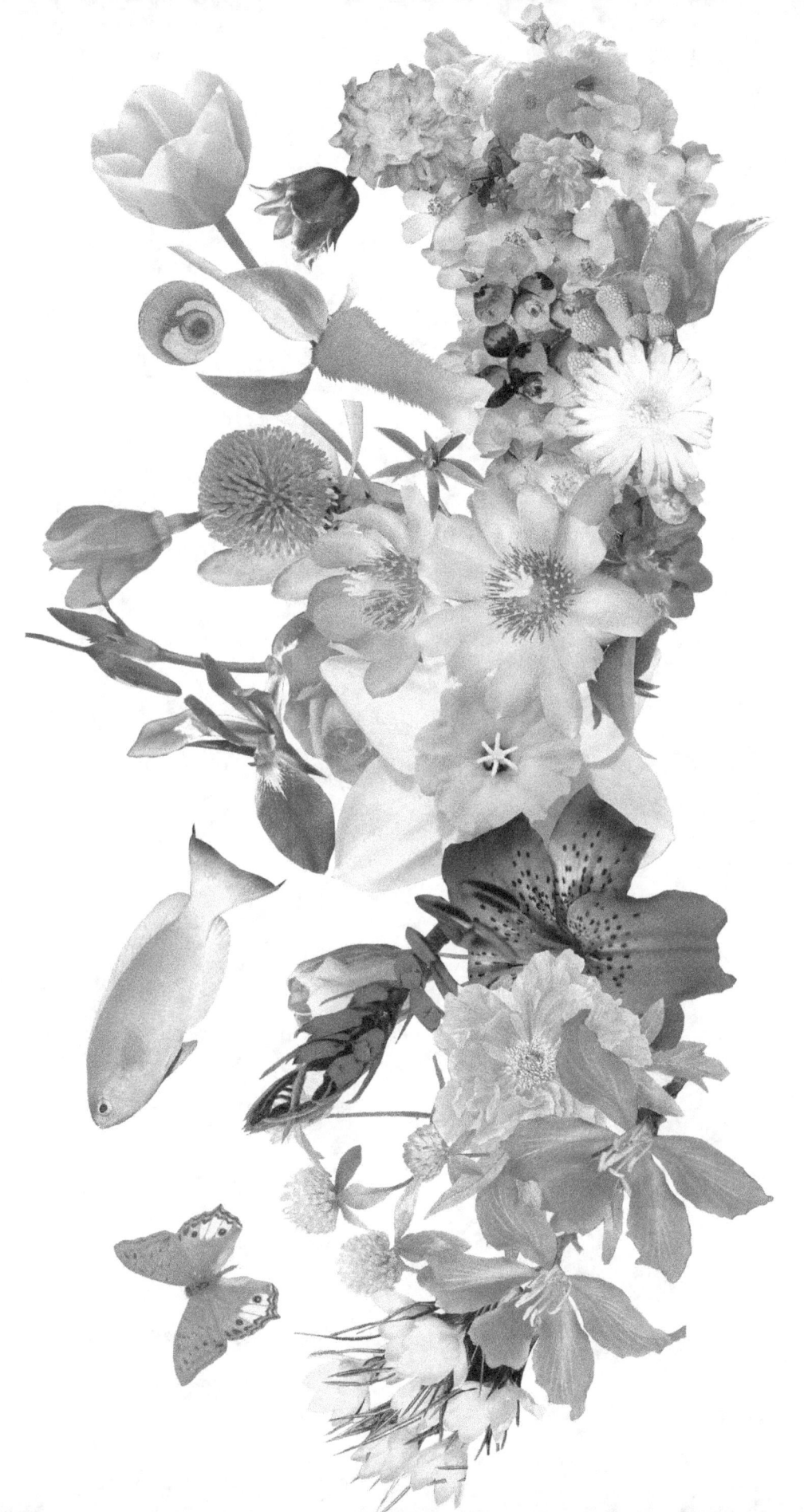

Kissing Pigs

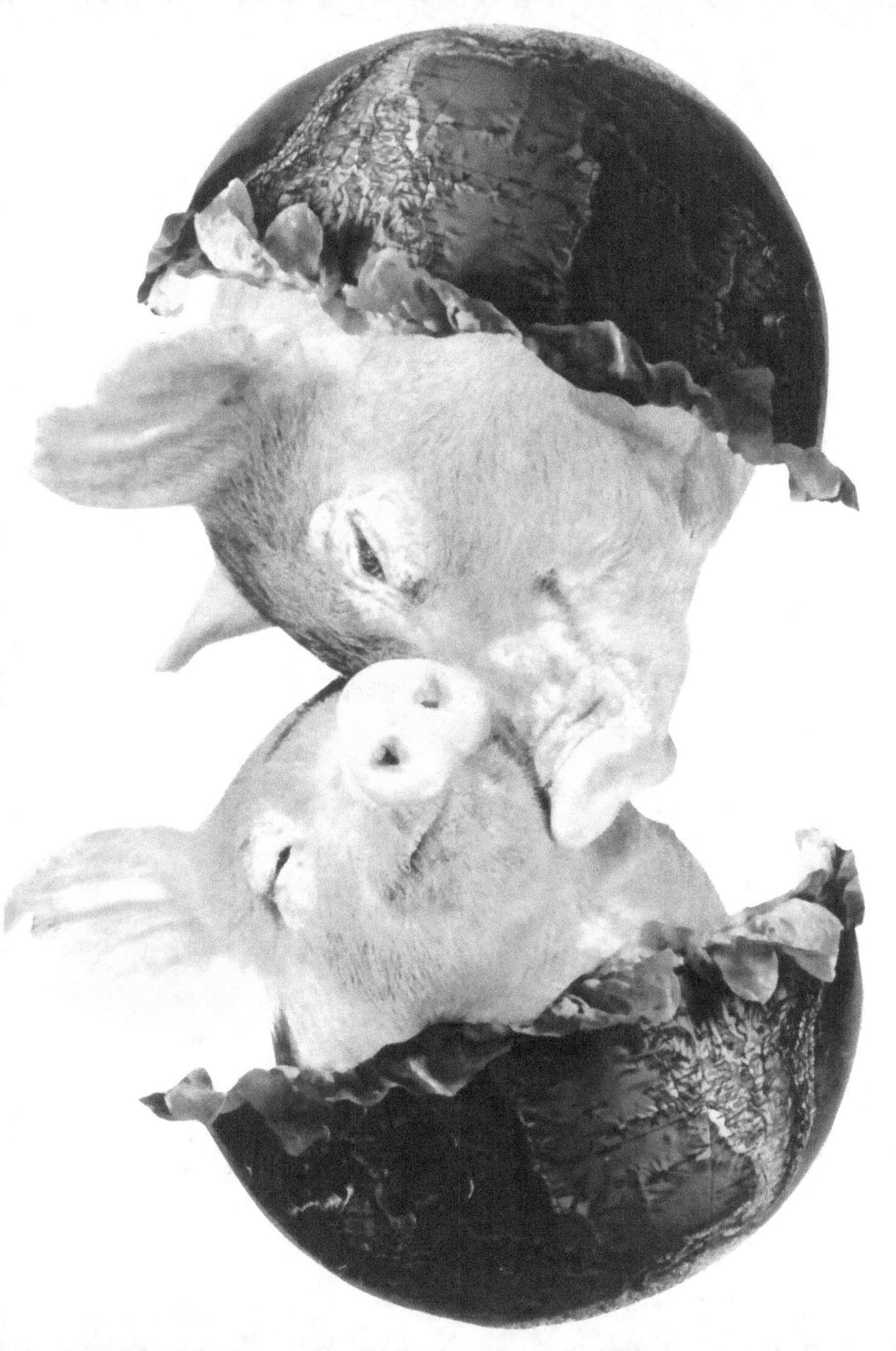

Lady in Waiting

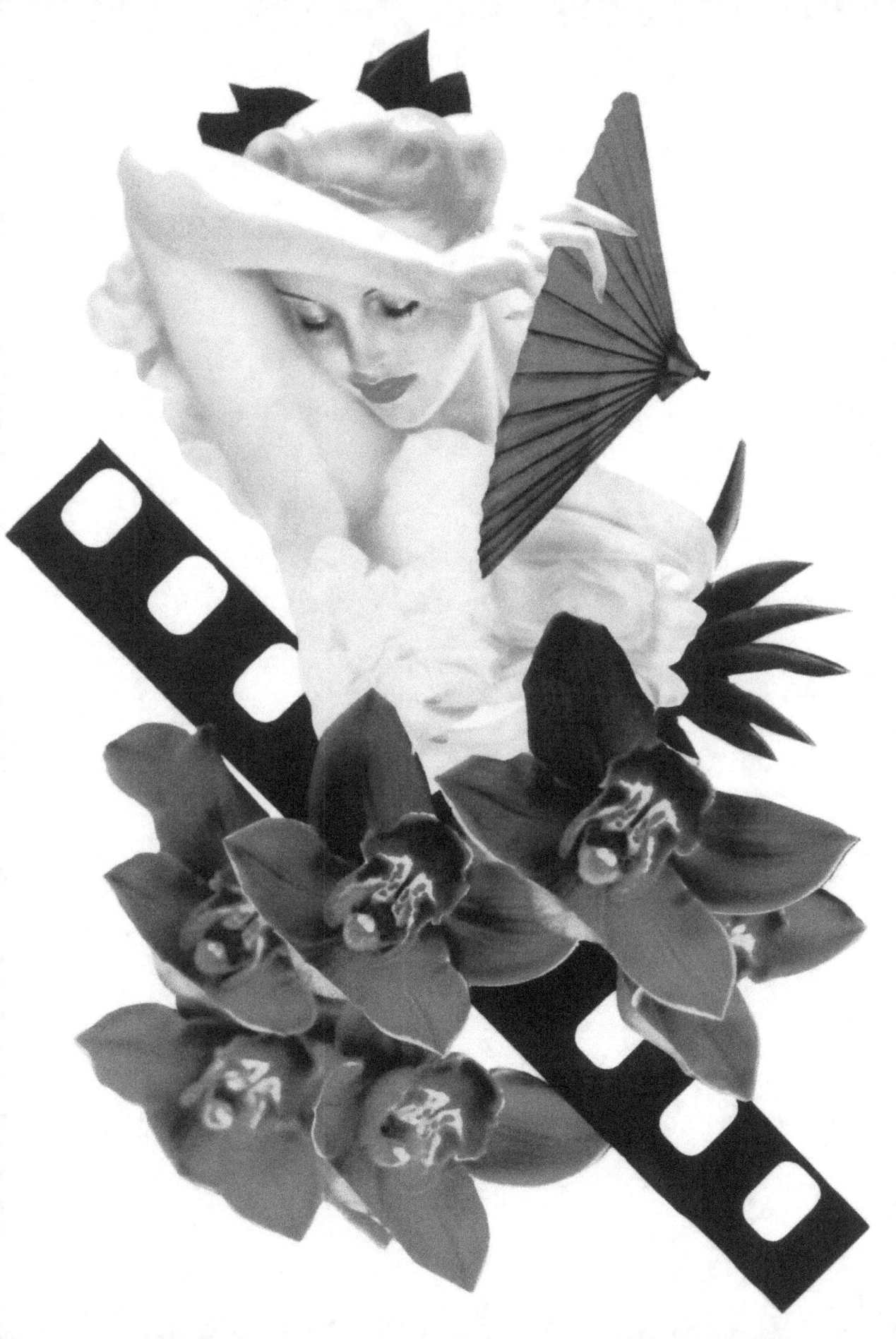

Lizard Garden

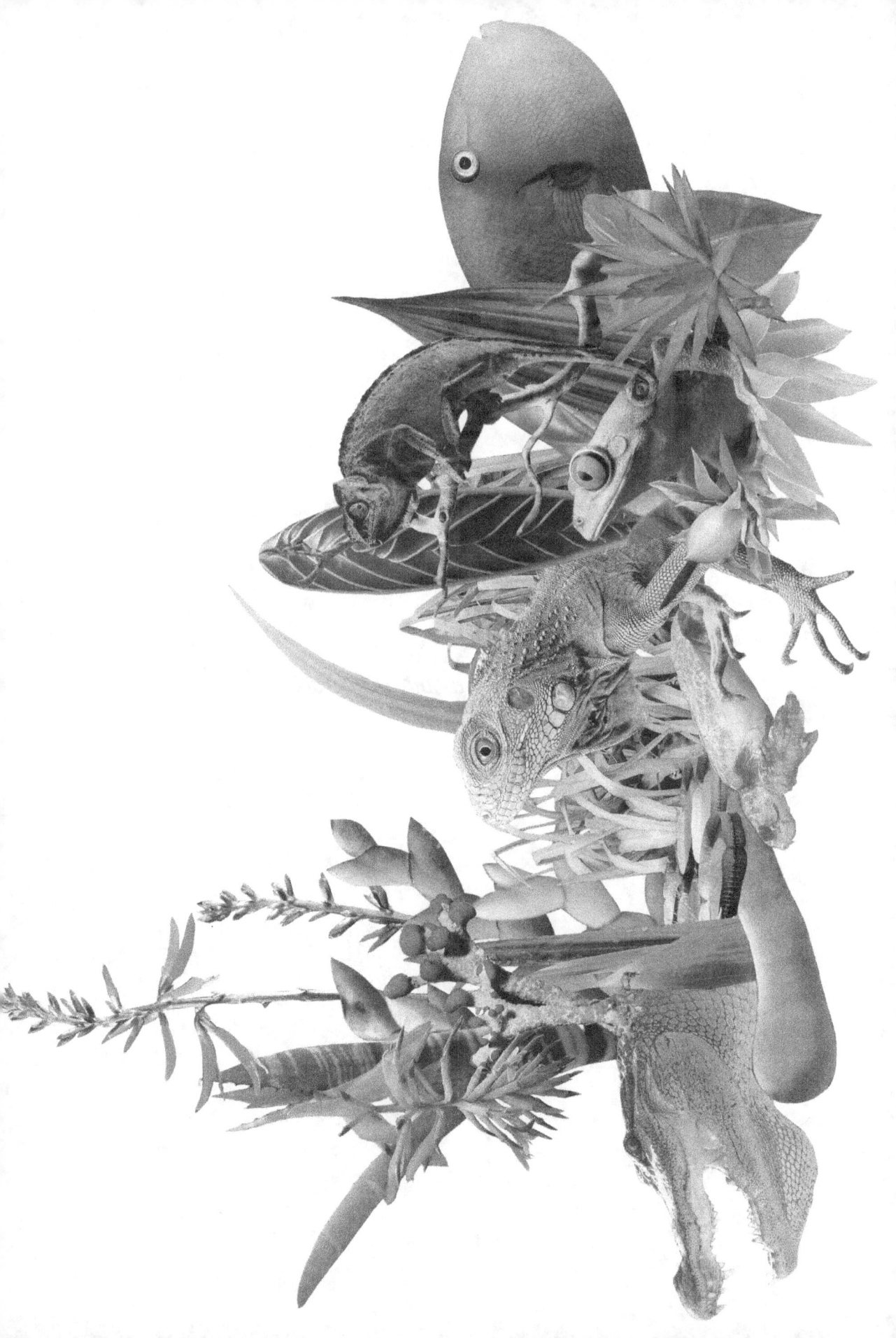

medicine man brewing psychedelics

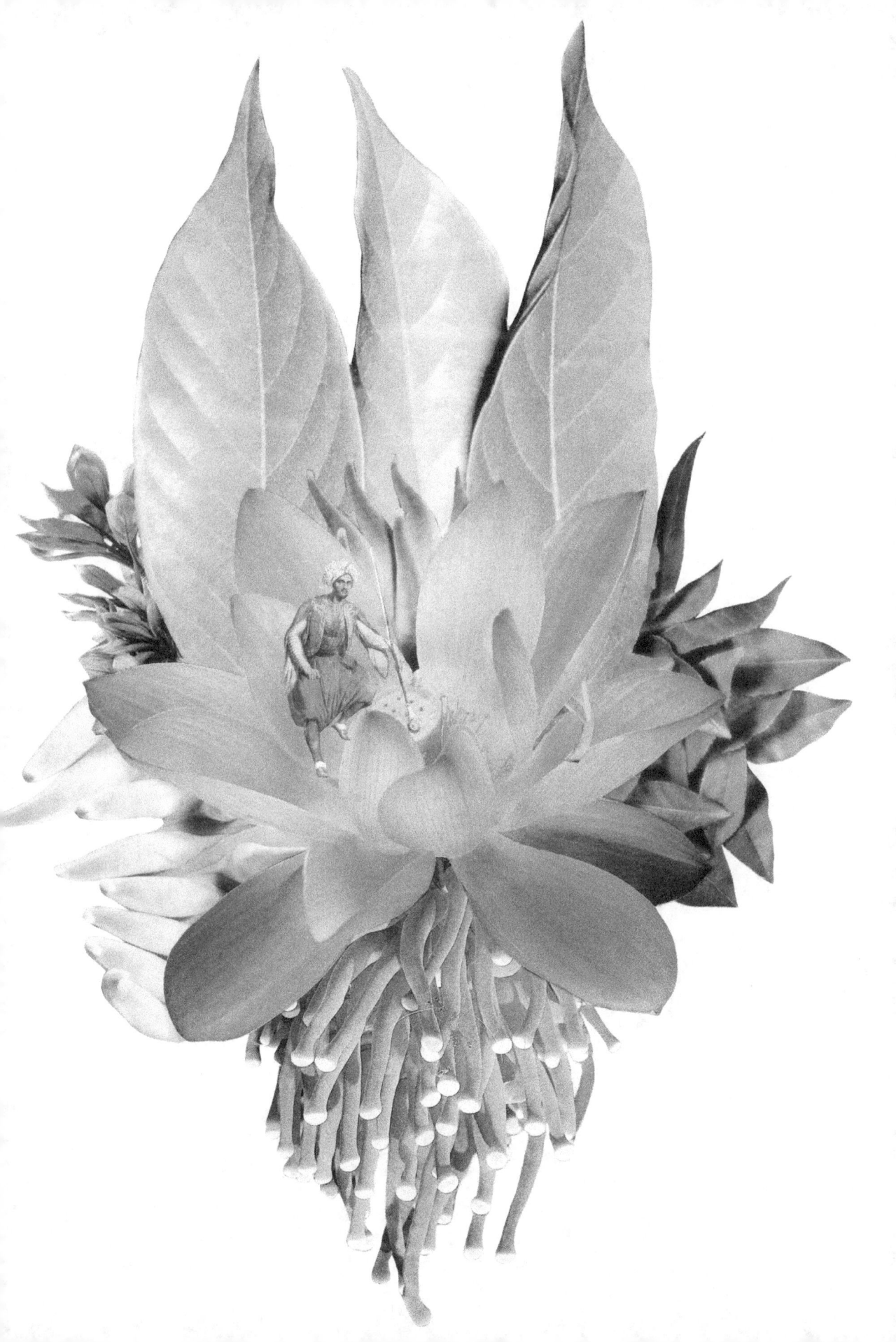

Milton Glaser's Lover

Milton Glaser's

Lover

Marsha Ross

Ollie and me

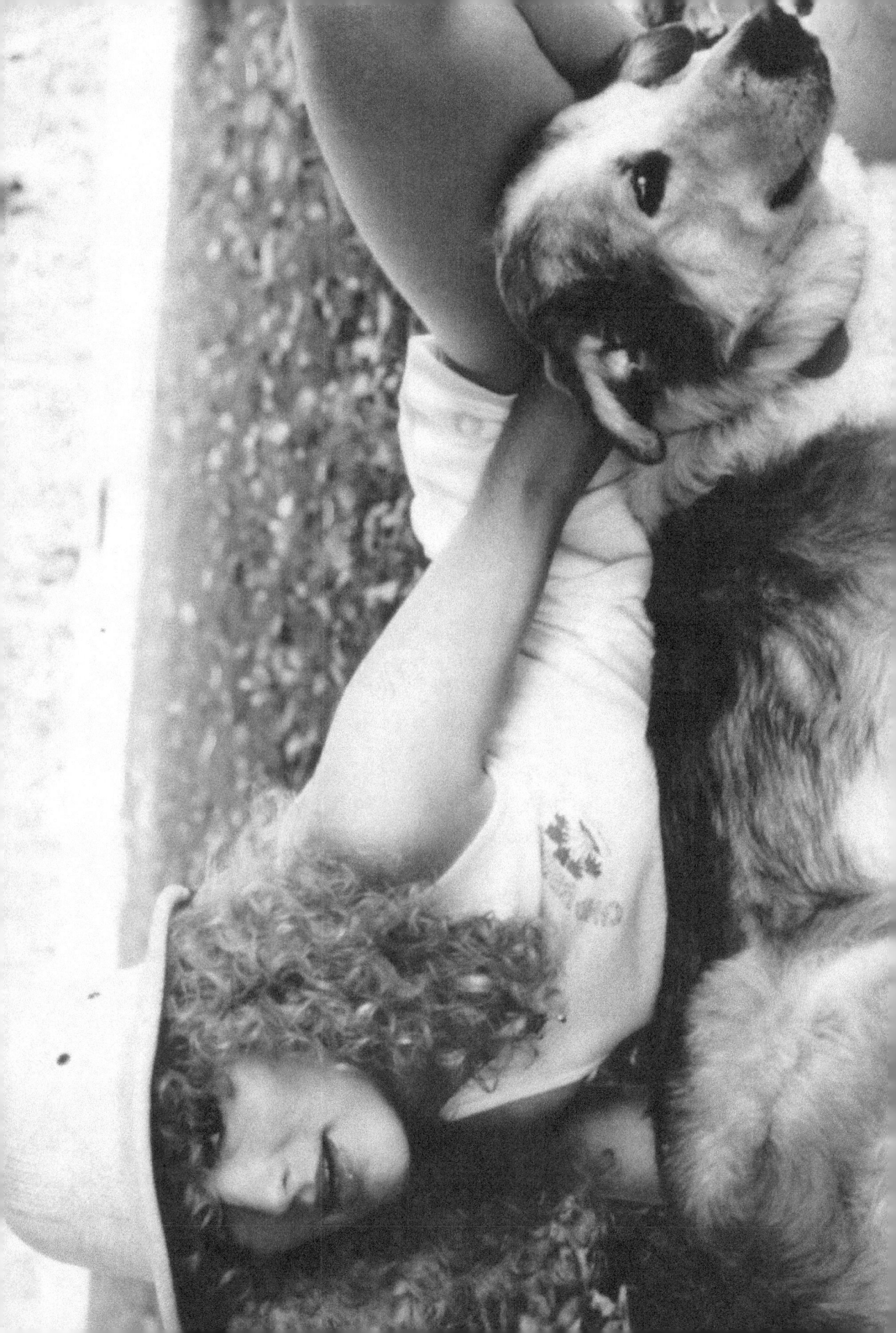

Opening Night

PHOTOSPHERE
Gallery of Photography

mon.	7 - 10 pm
tues.	1 - 6 pm
wed.	1 - 6 pm
thurs.	1 - 6 pm
fri. - sat.	4 - 10 pm

8222 Sunset Boulevard
Los Angeles, California 90046

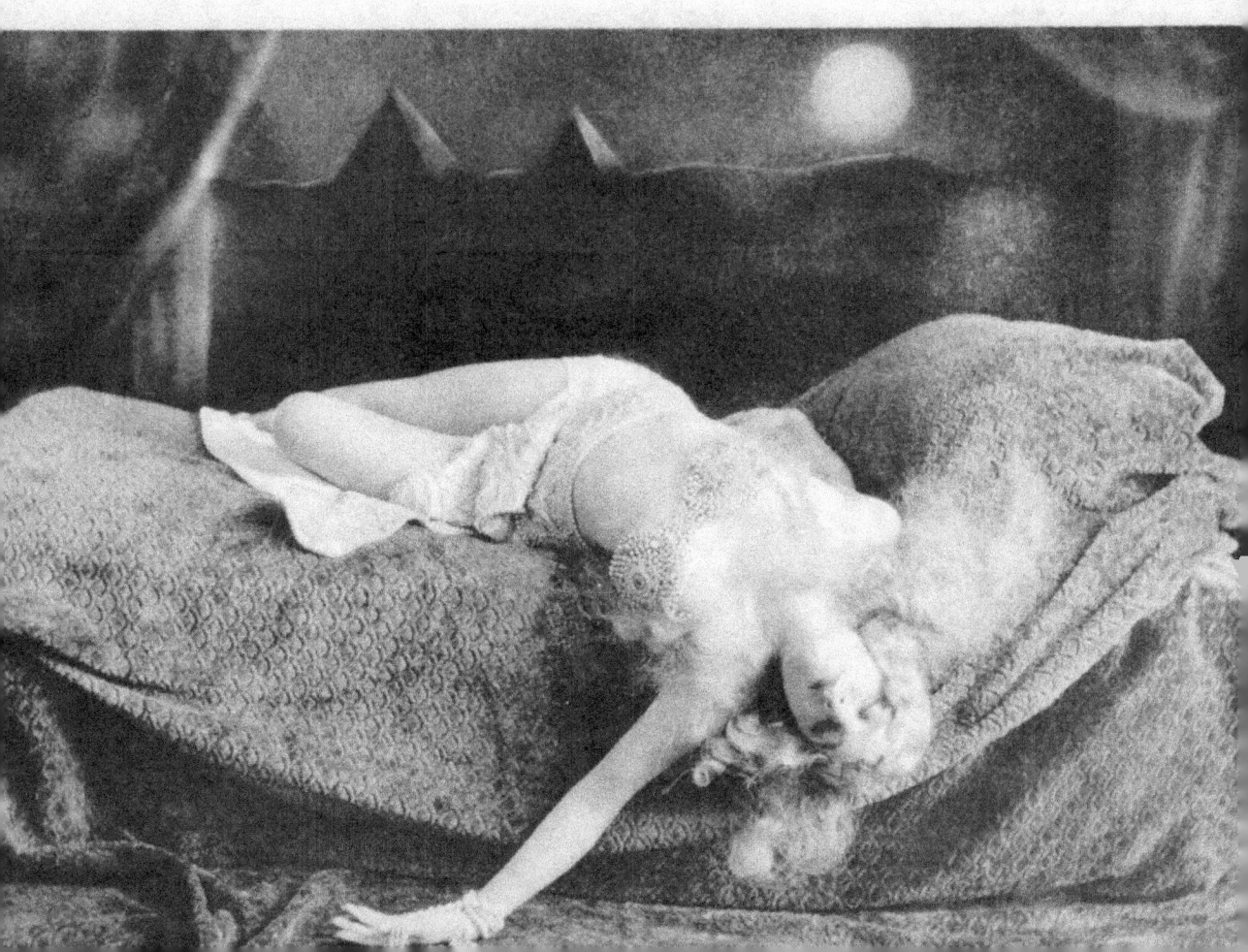

Orange Buddah

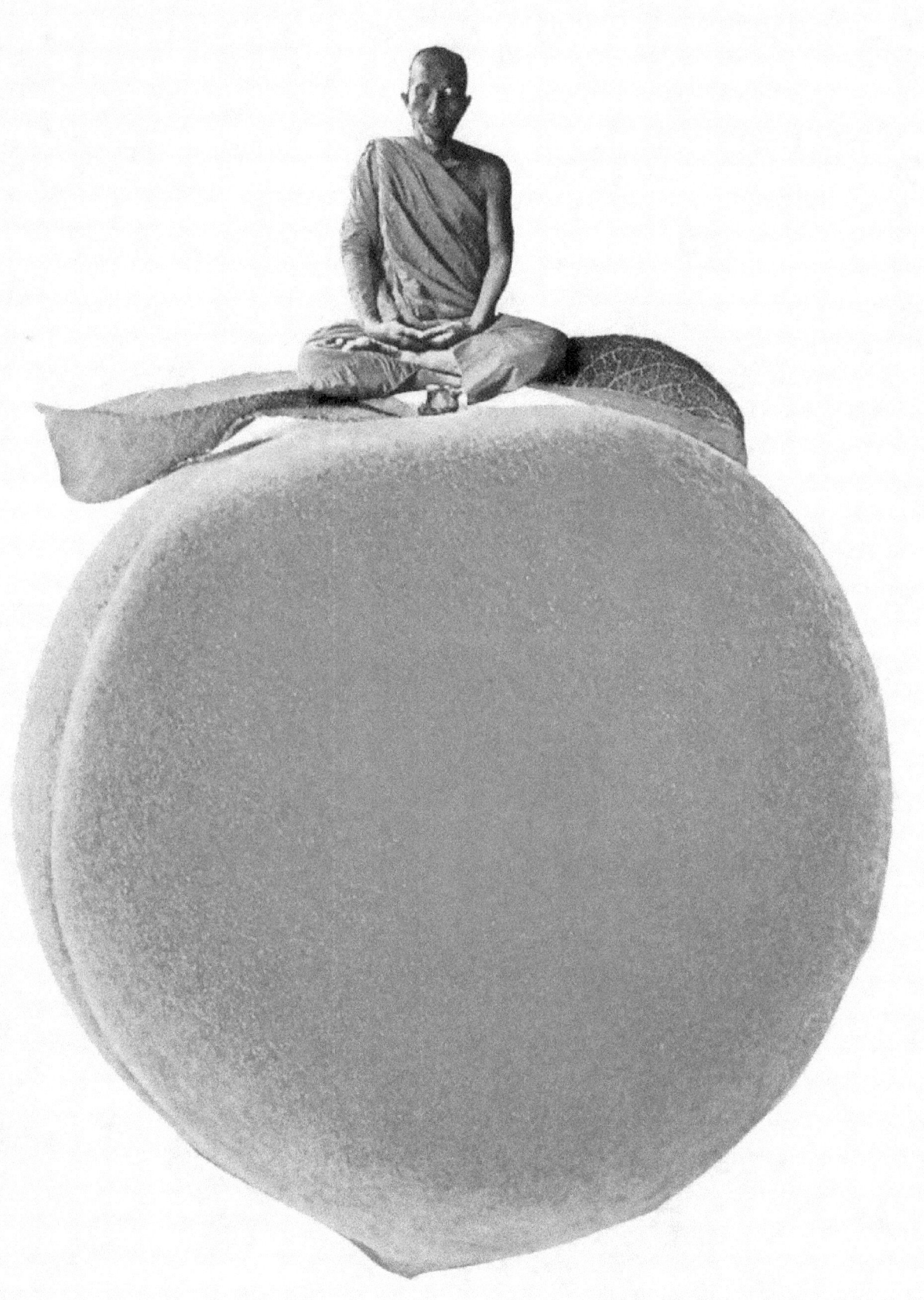

My Heart

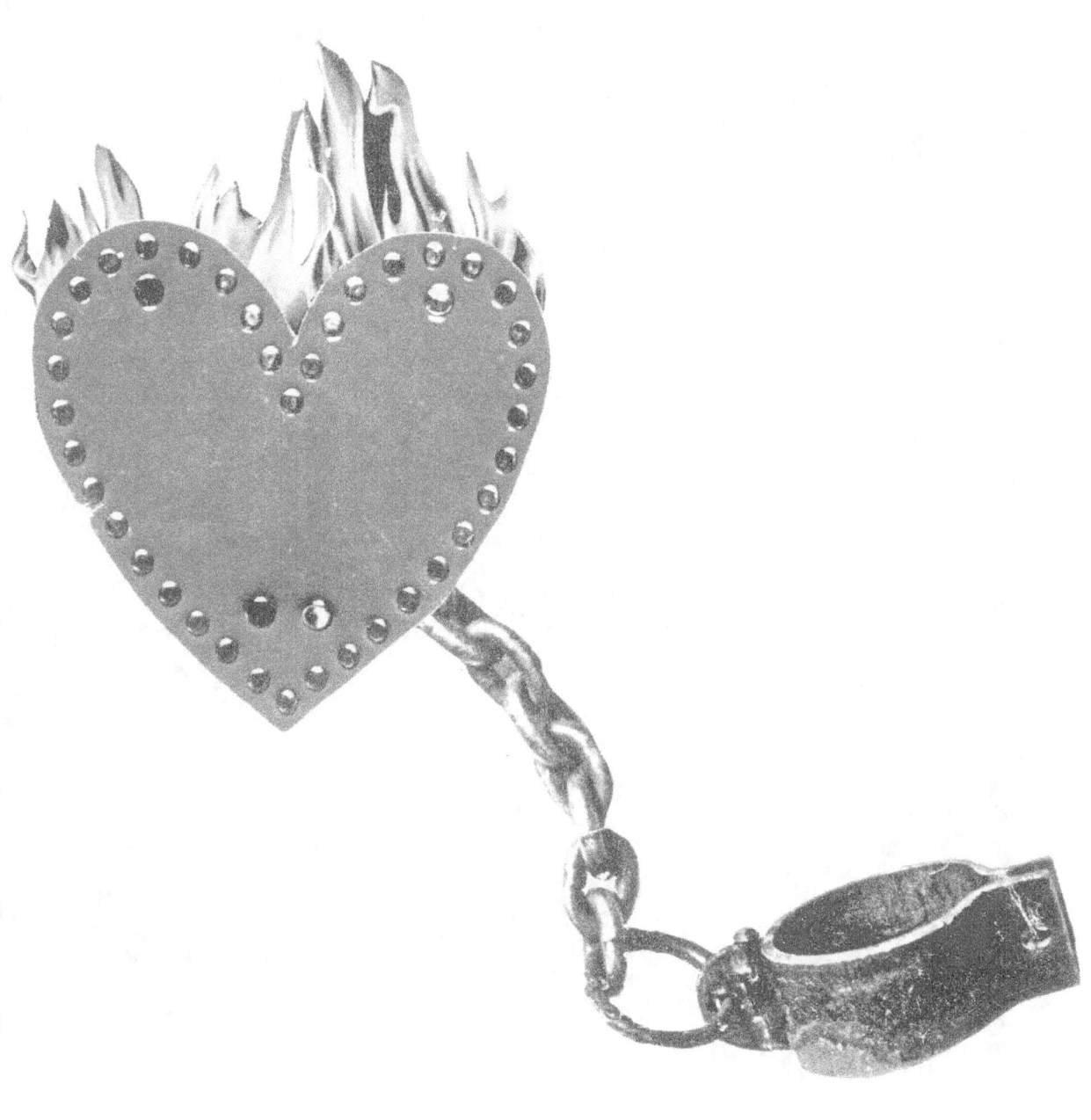

underwater creatures

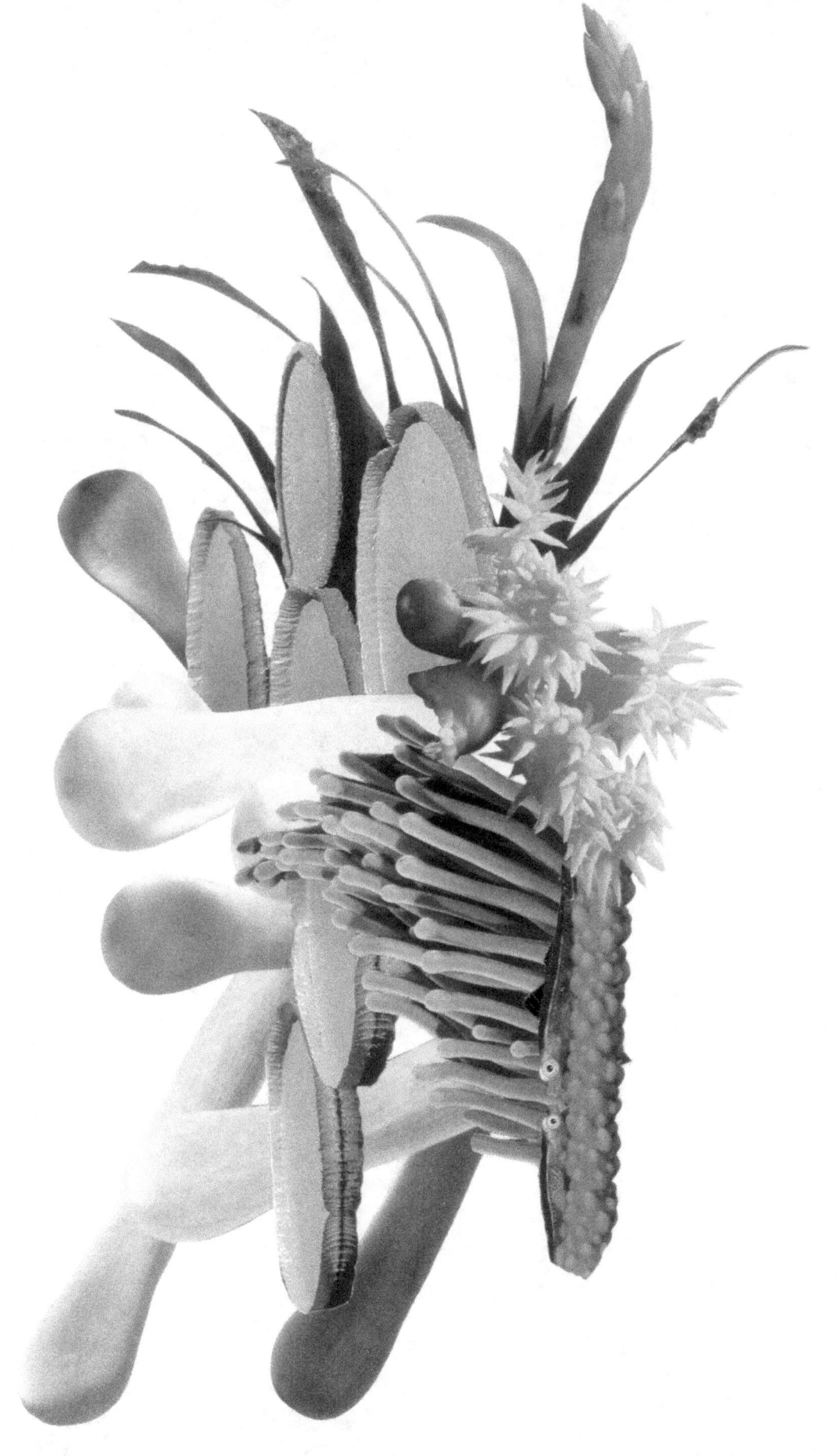

lotus love

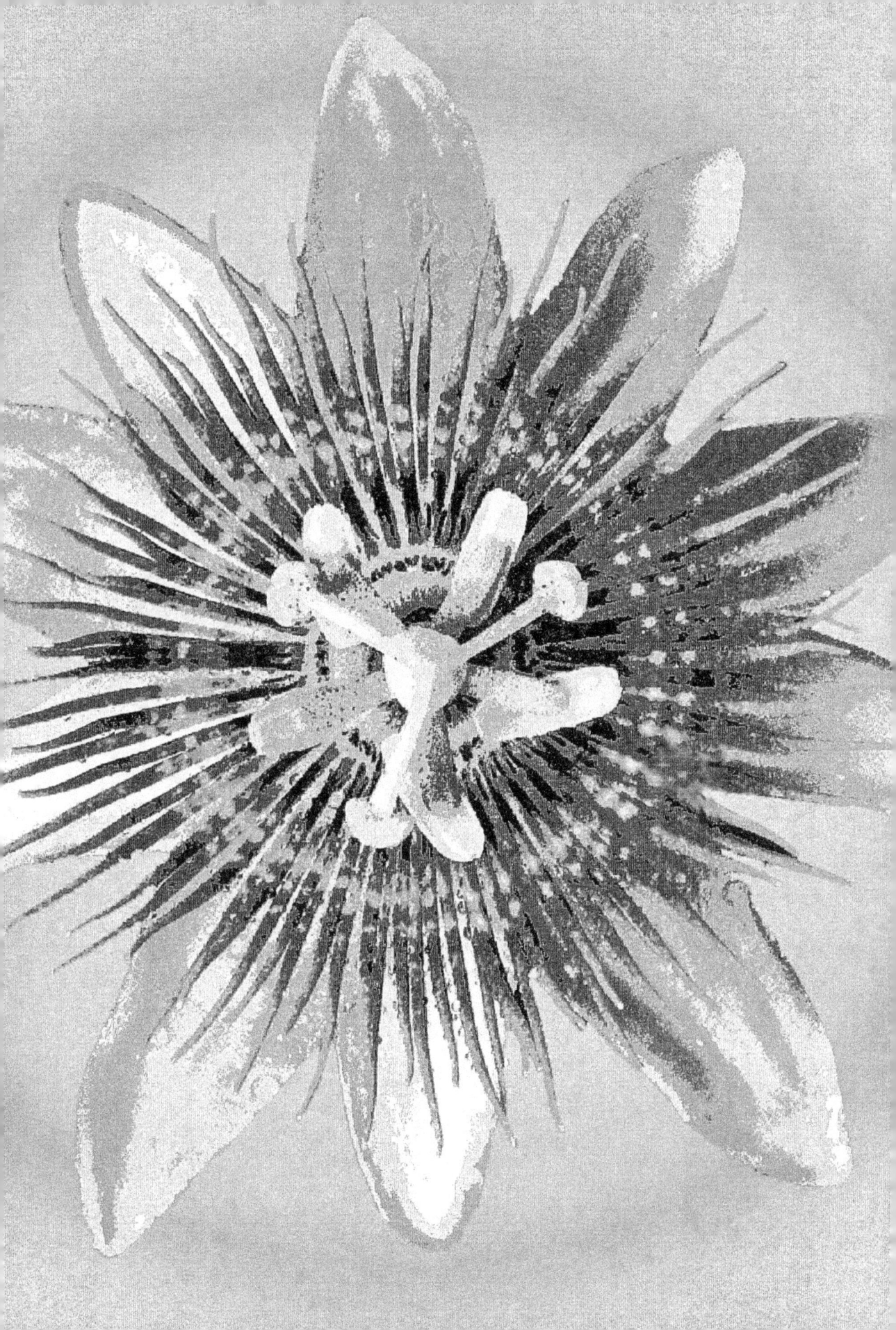

tiger tops

No electricity but everyday we rode elephants
for four hours exploring the Game Preserve
in Nrpal

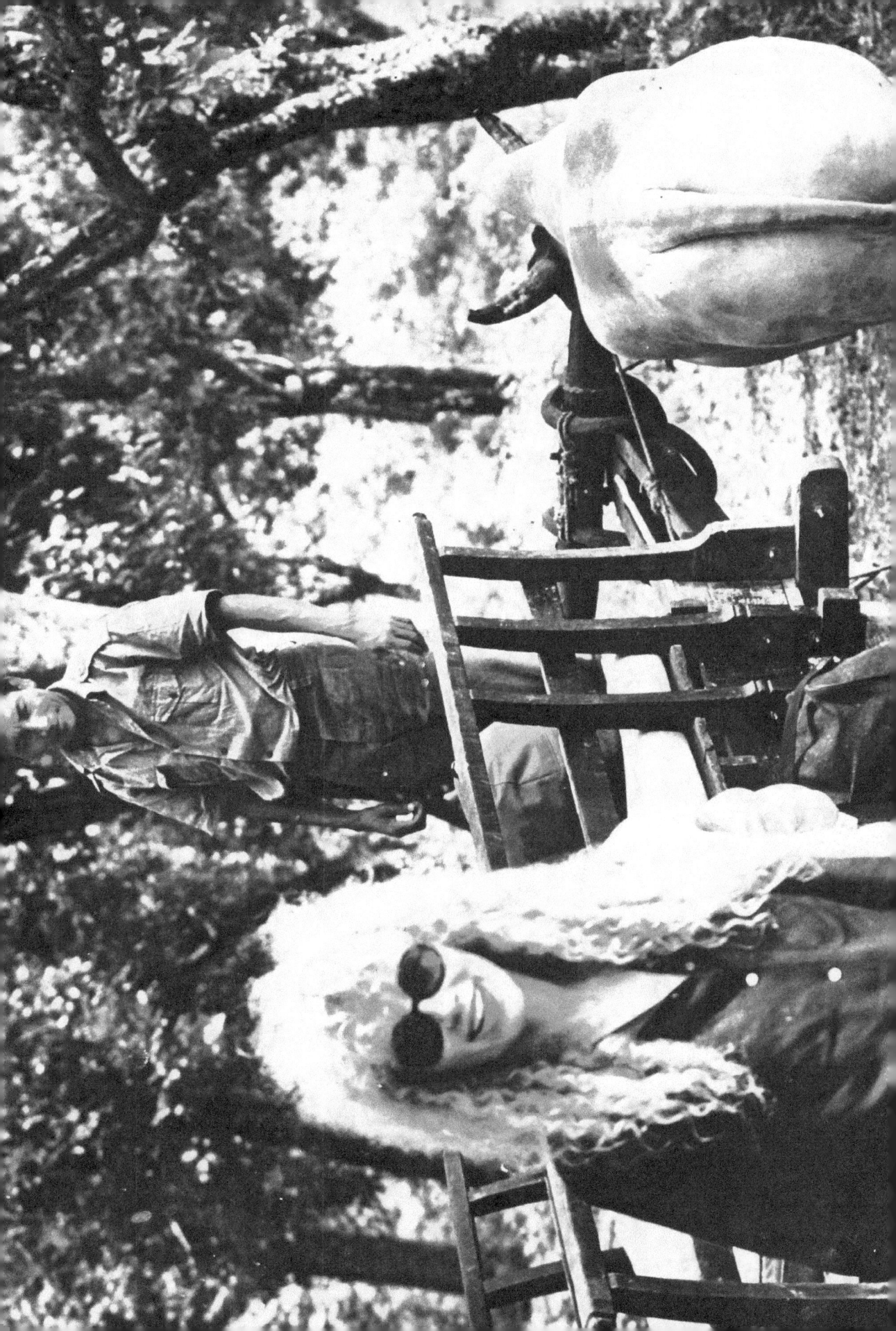

A new Dali...?

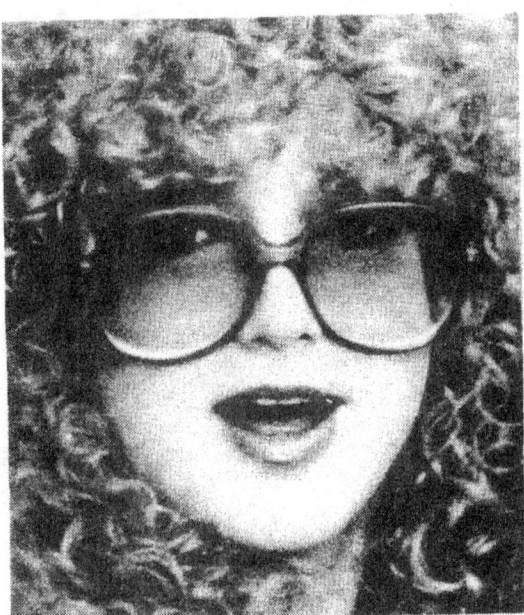

Hollywood producer **Marsha Ross** has been hailed in Cannes as a new **Salvador Dali** with her multimedia art collection which satirizes American presidents, rock music and Hollywood.

Her outrageous imagery, titled Inside Hollywood, will open in the movie capital in late June when she returns from Cannes where she's negotiating with European financiers for film backing.

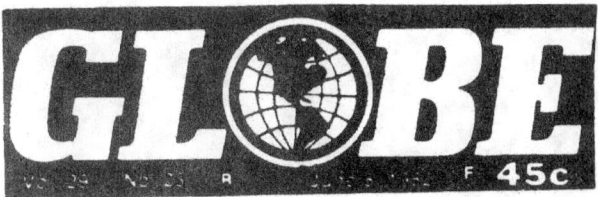

GLOBE F 45c

Burma monks

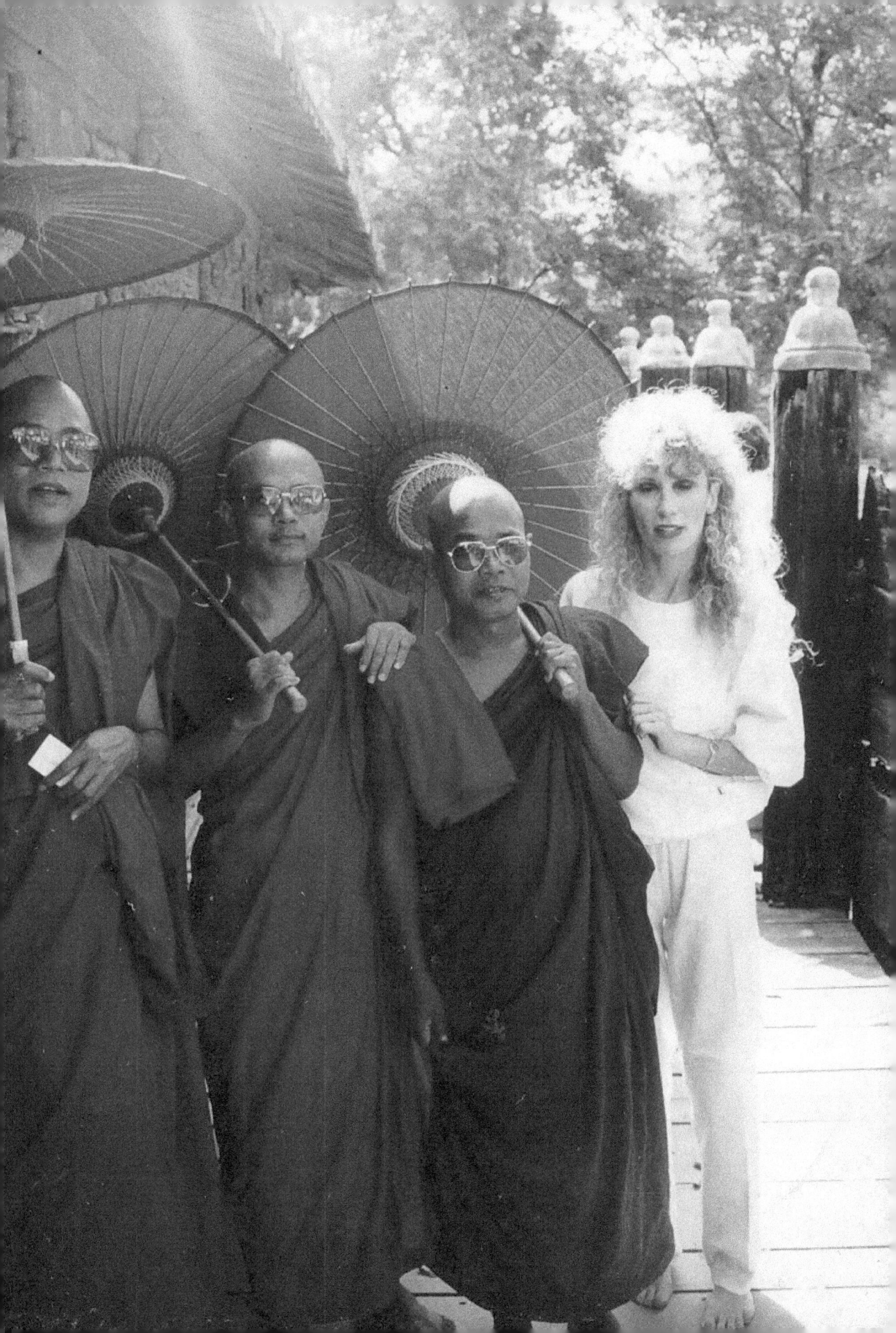

Columbe D'or in Saint Paul de Vence
While at Cannes Film Festival

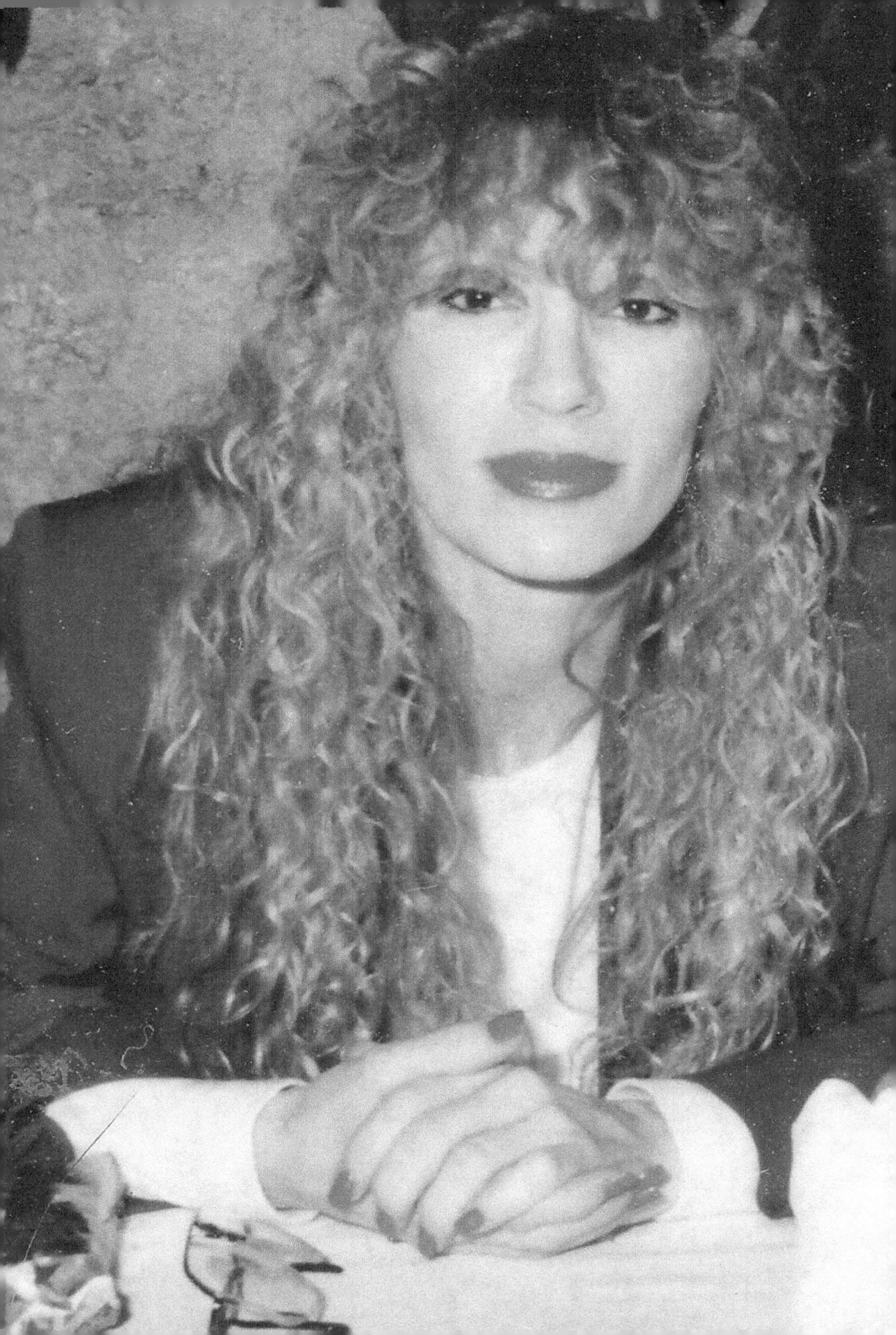

Flamingo Love

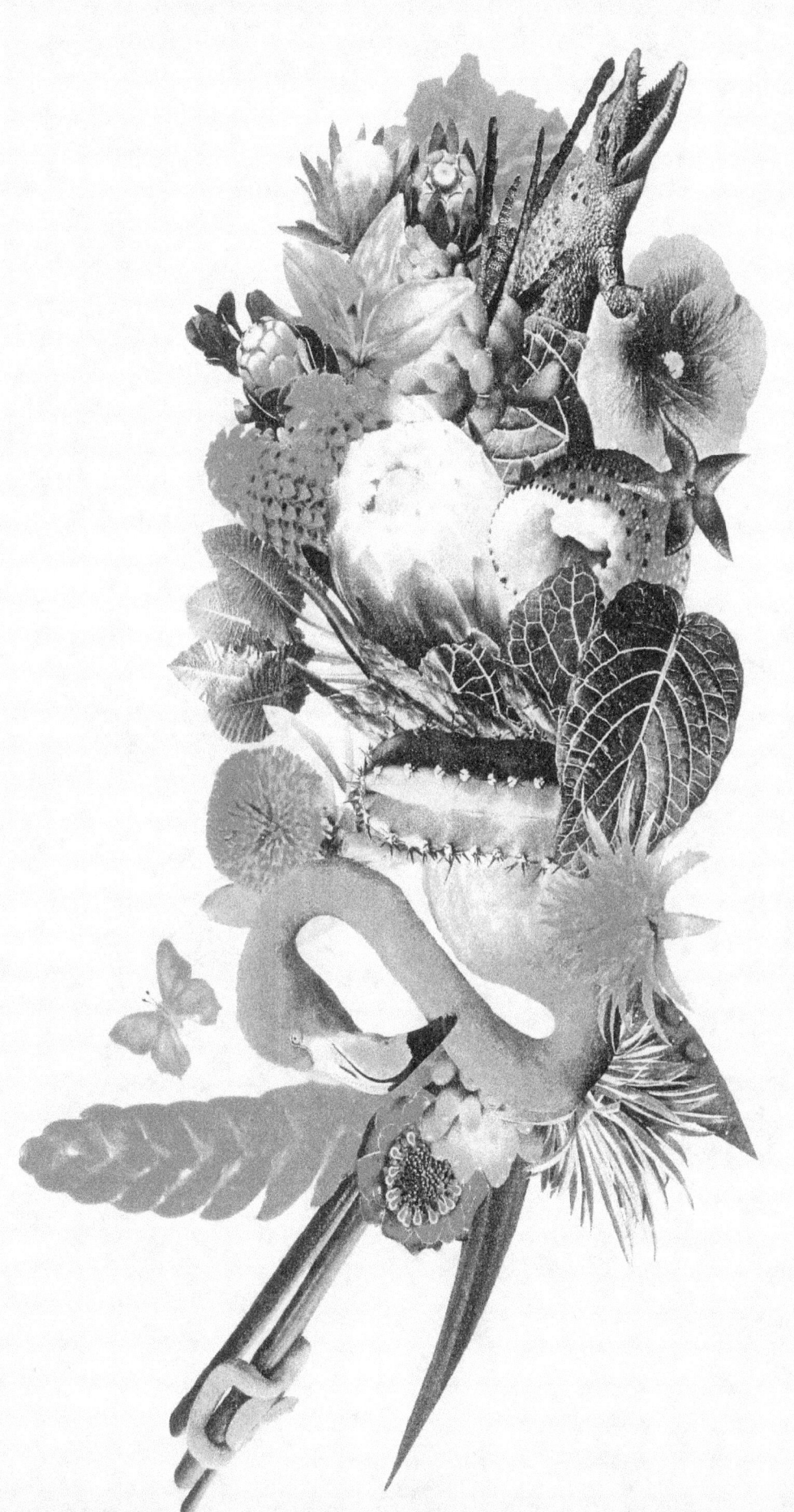

Fuzzy Flowers

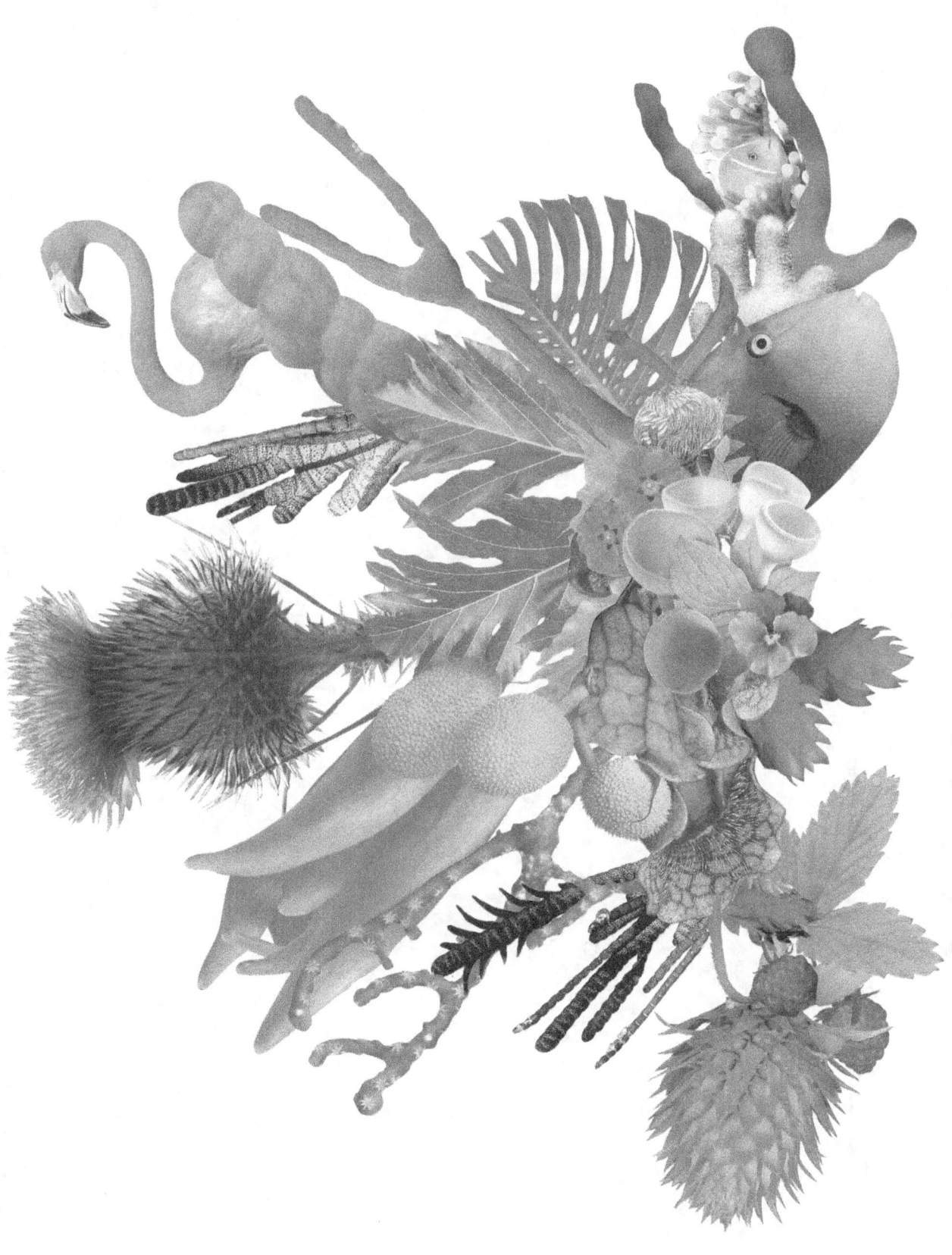

Ganesh

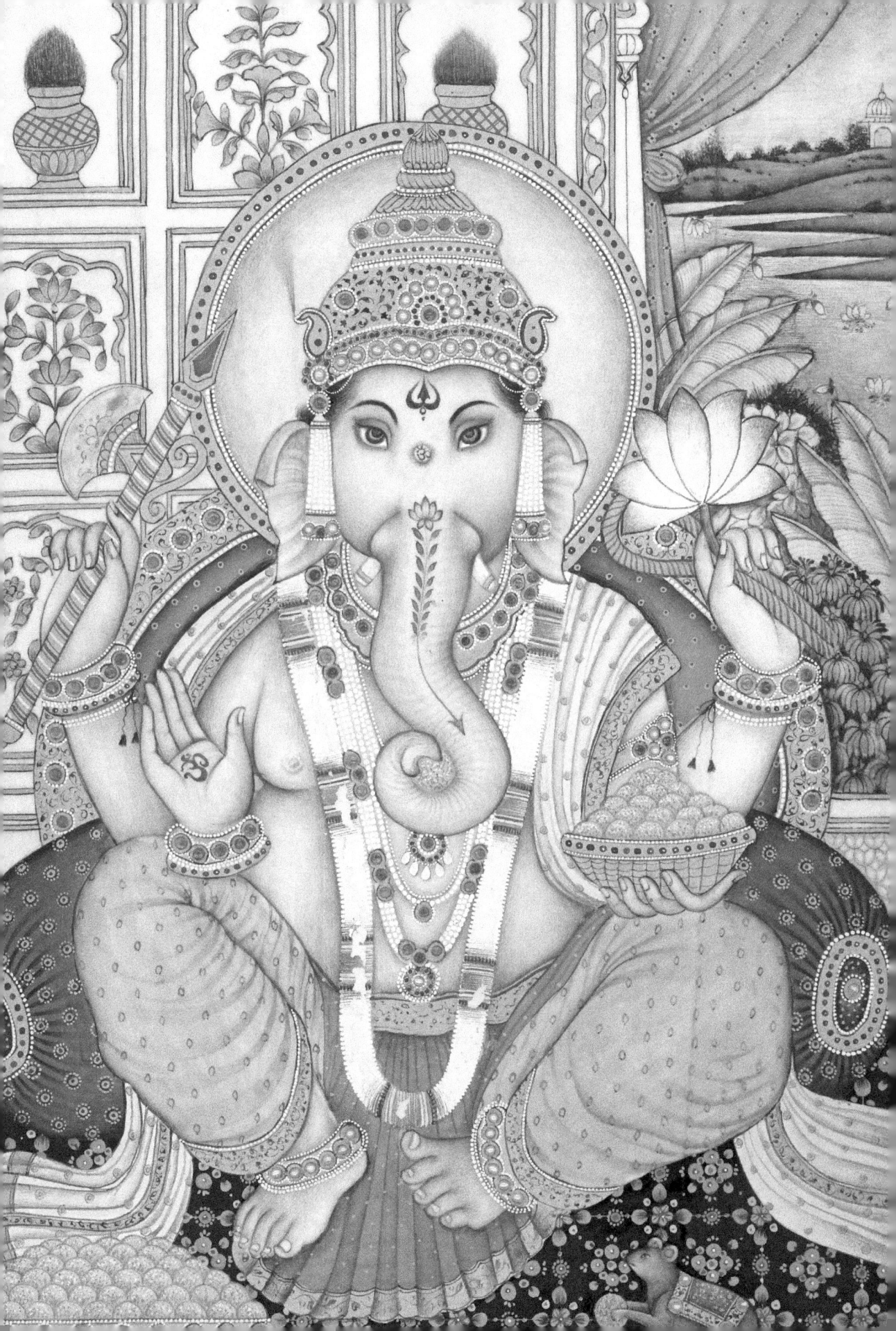

Girl in Garden

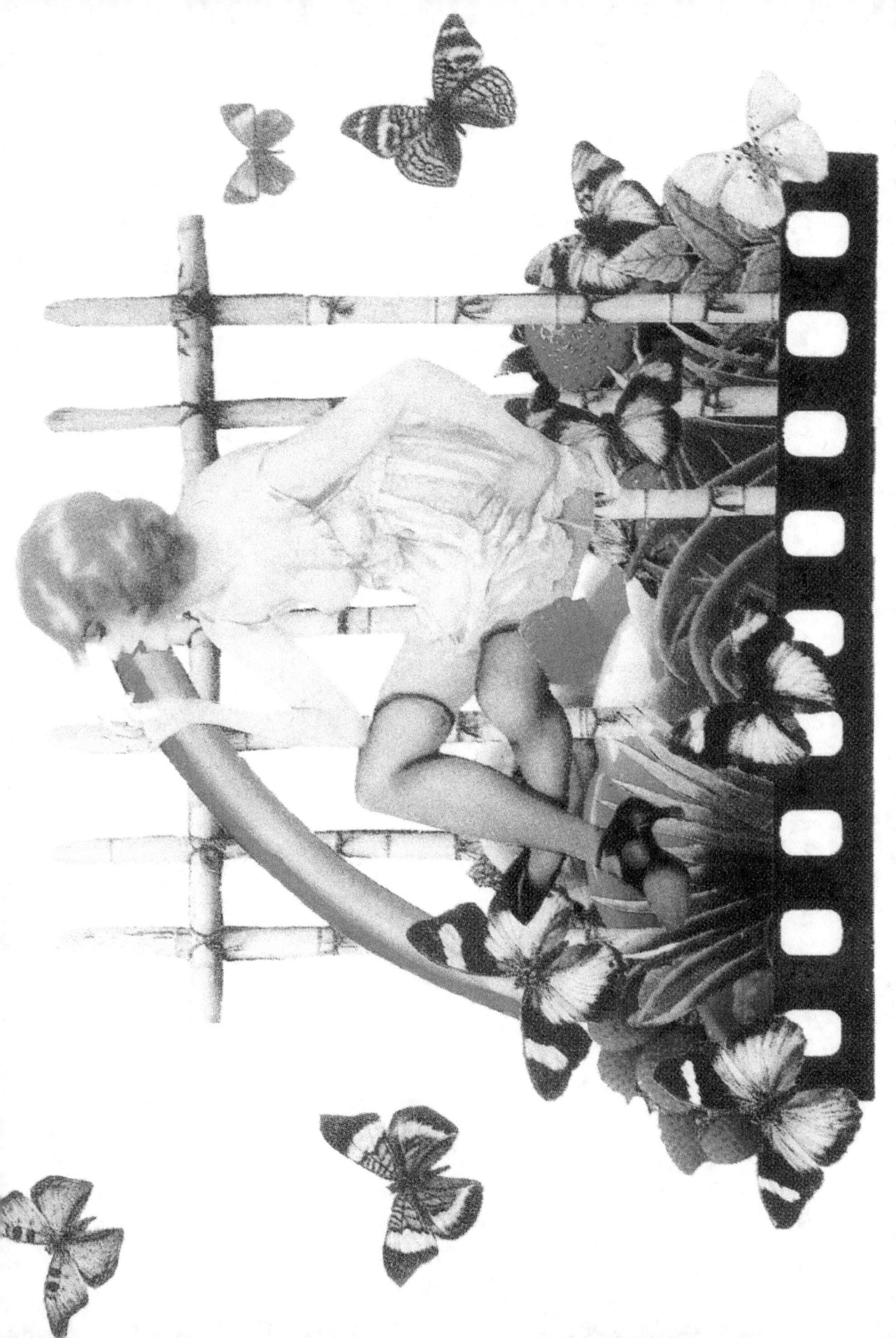

at a party in my living room

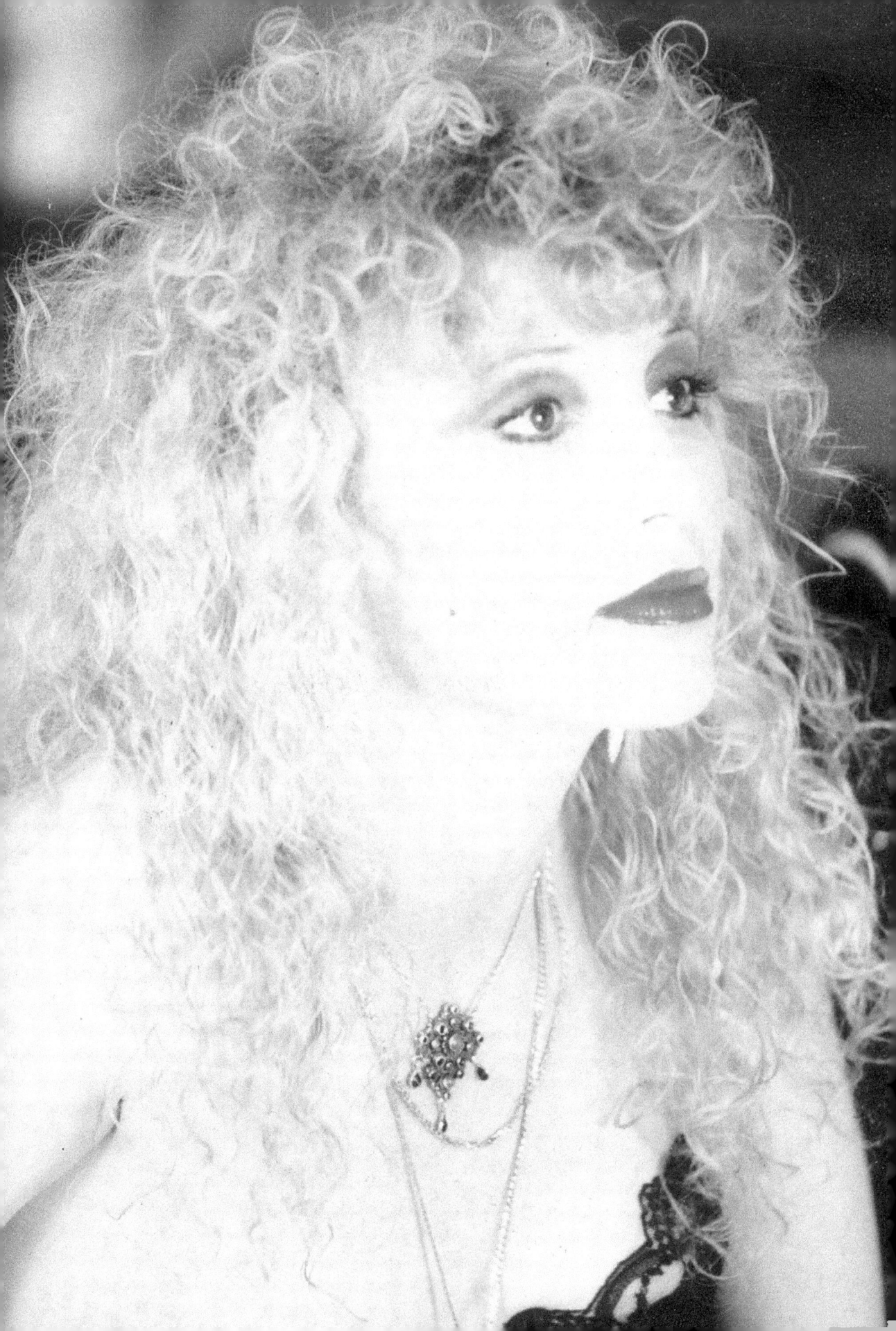

Jungle Heaven

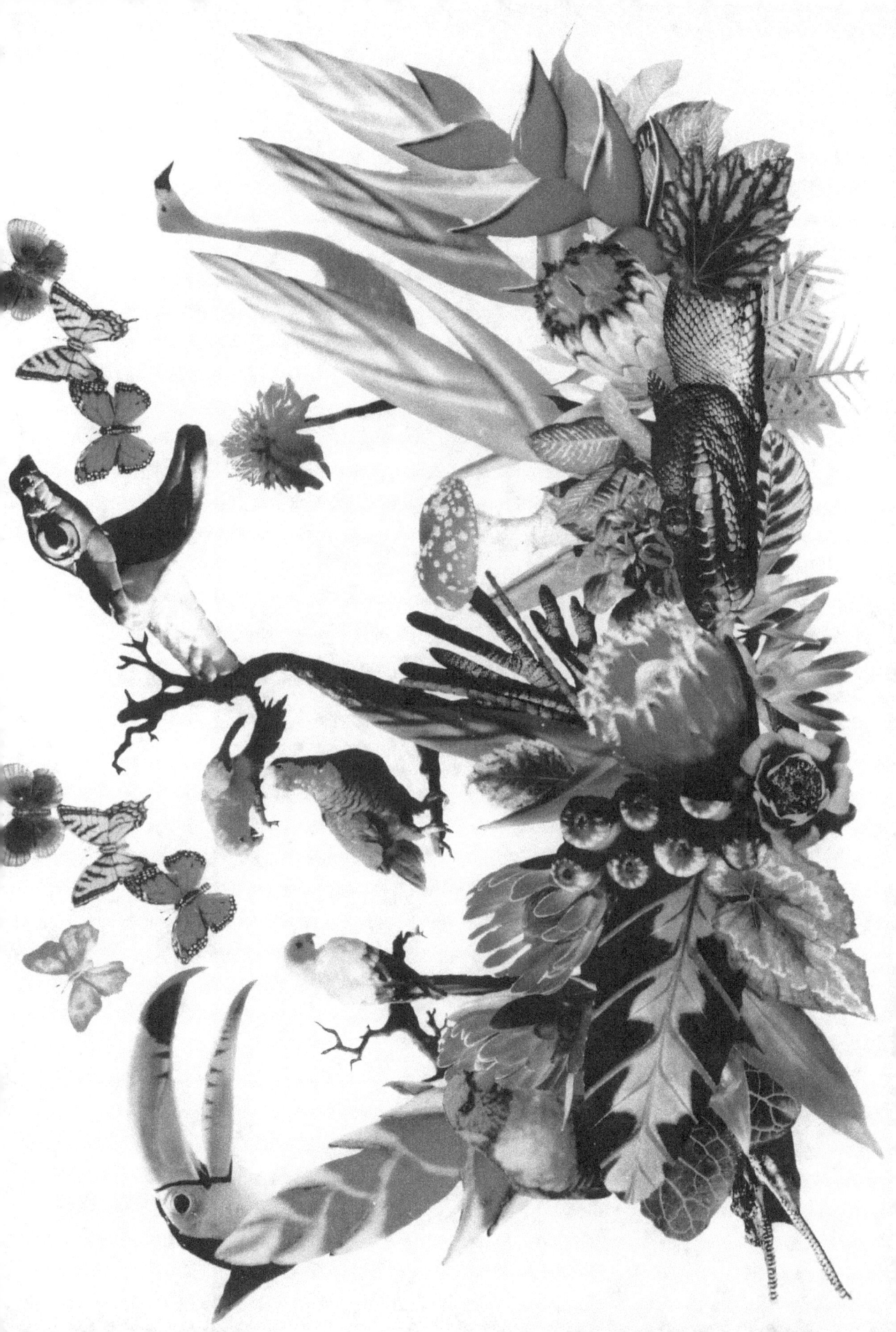

Kissing Sweetie

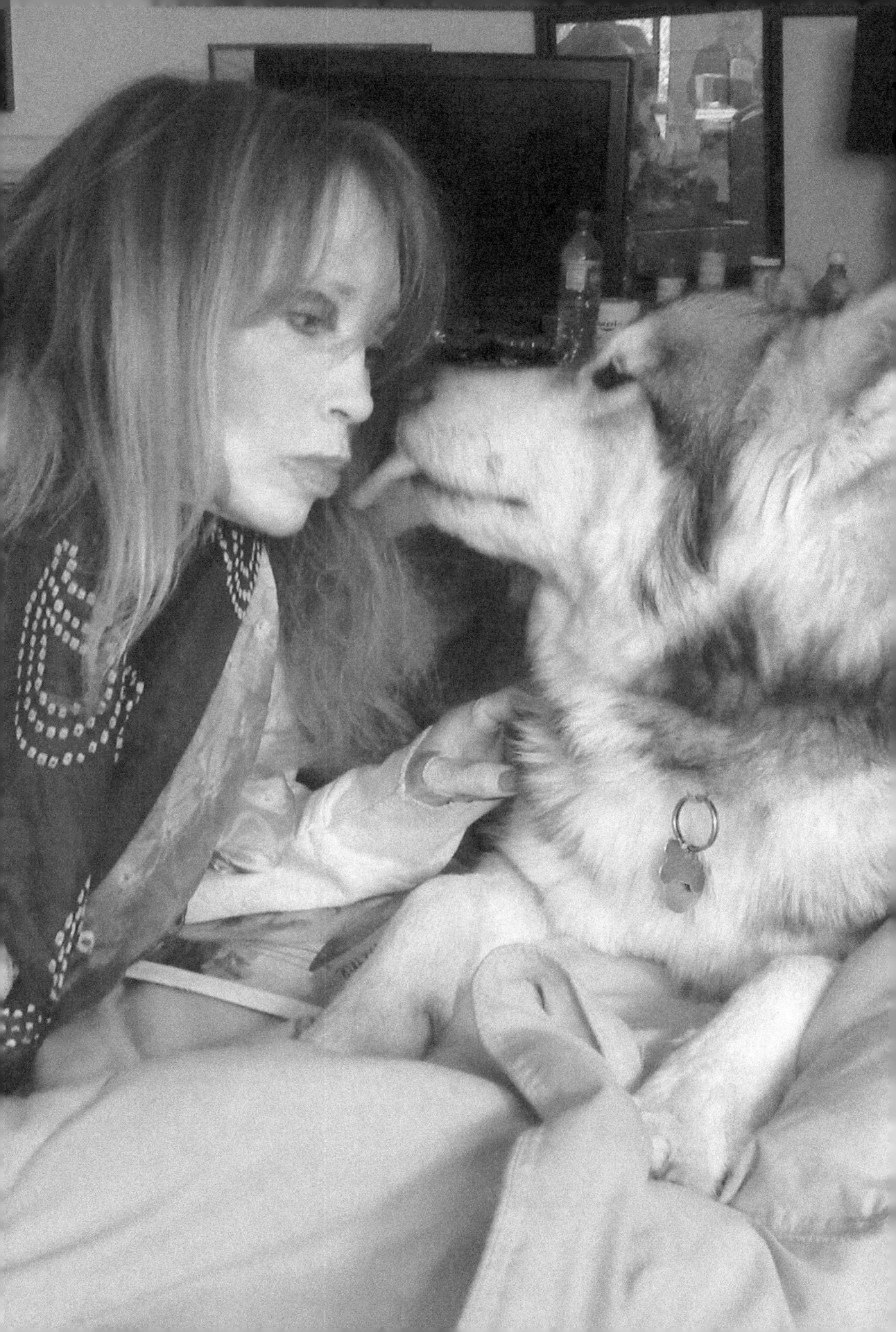

I am on a camel deep in the Sahara

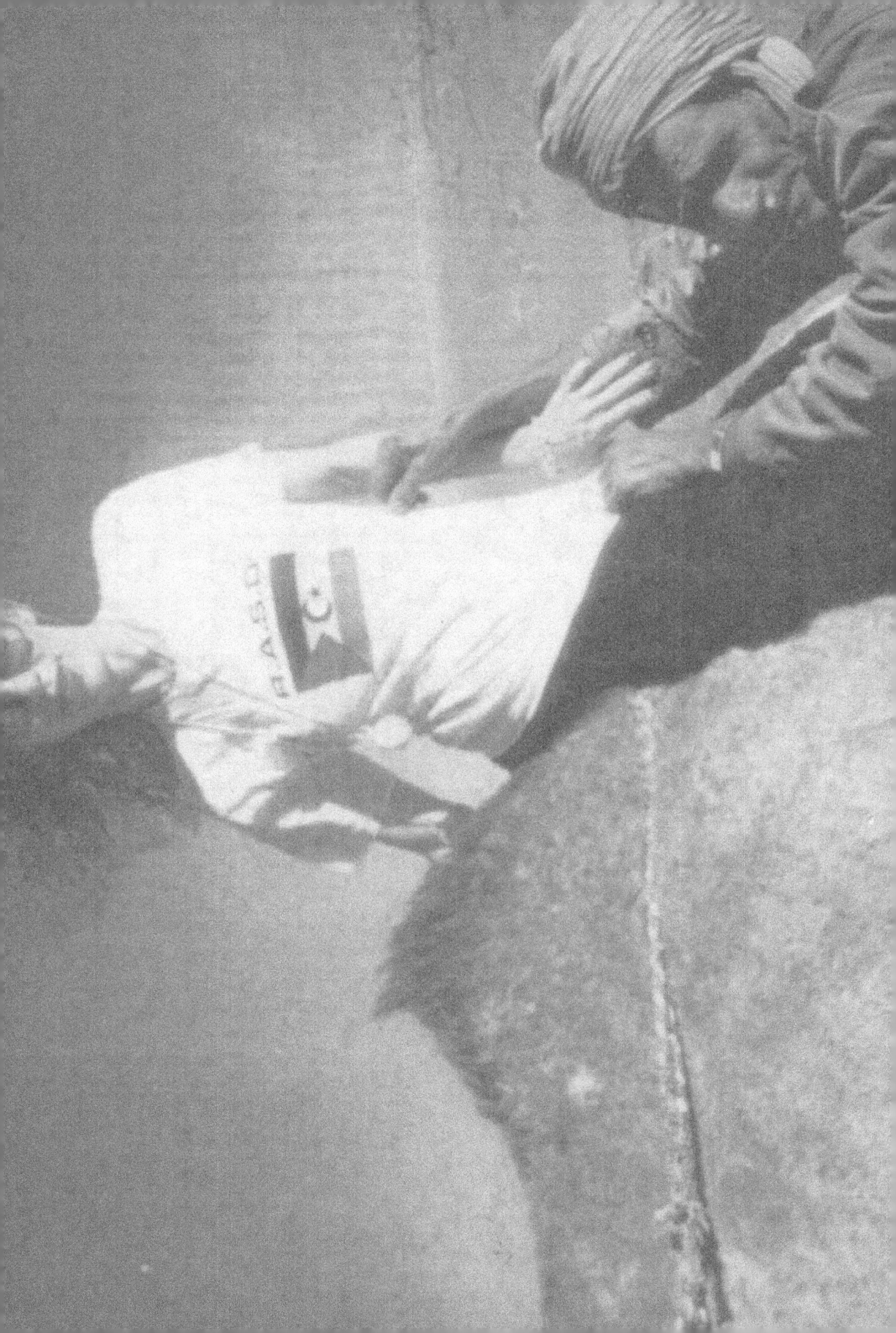

Parrot Burst

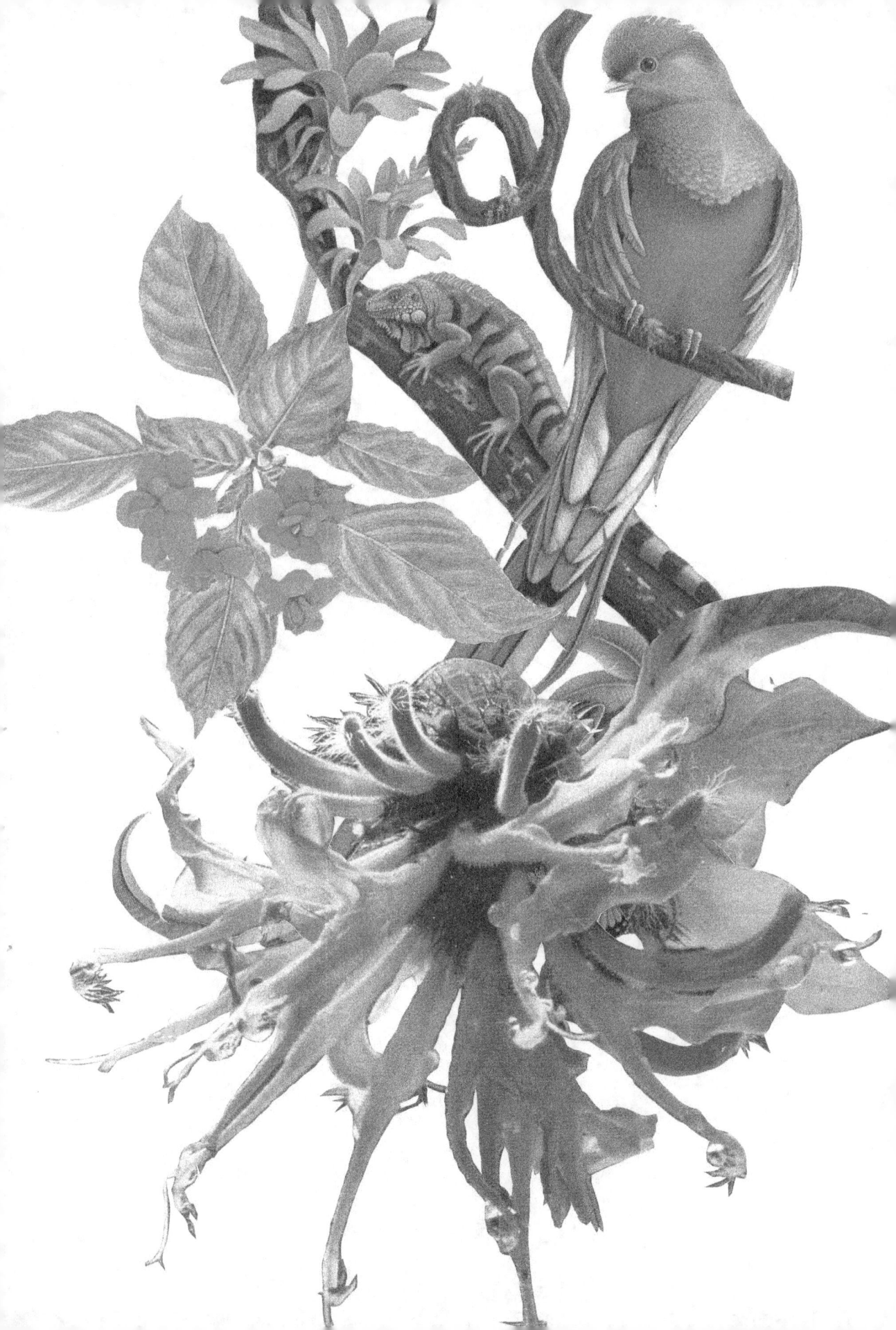

Photosphere Poster

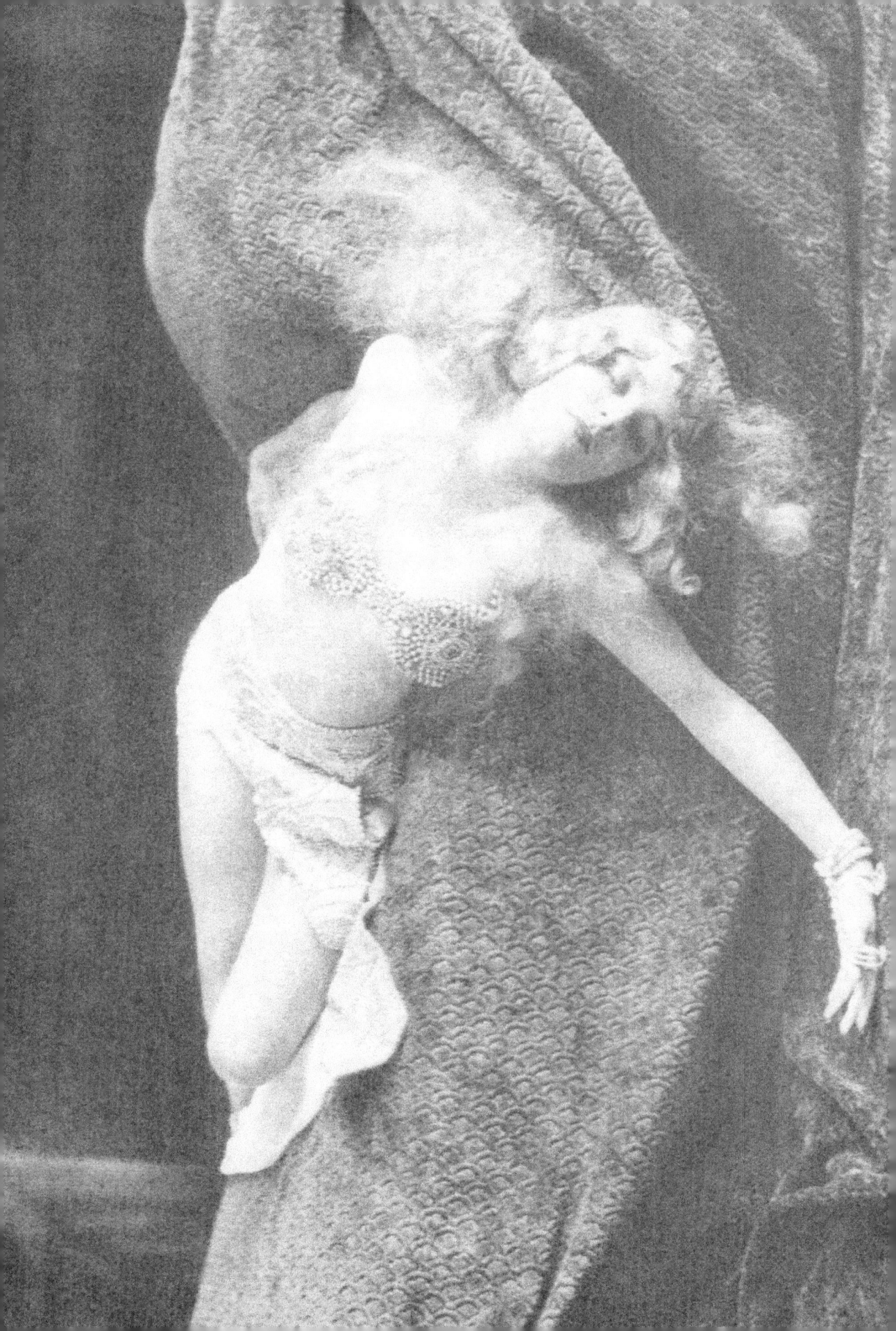

Polosario Camels in the Sahara

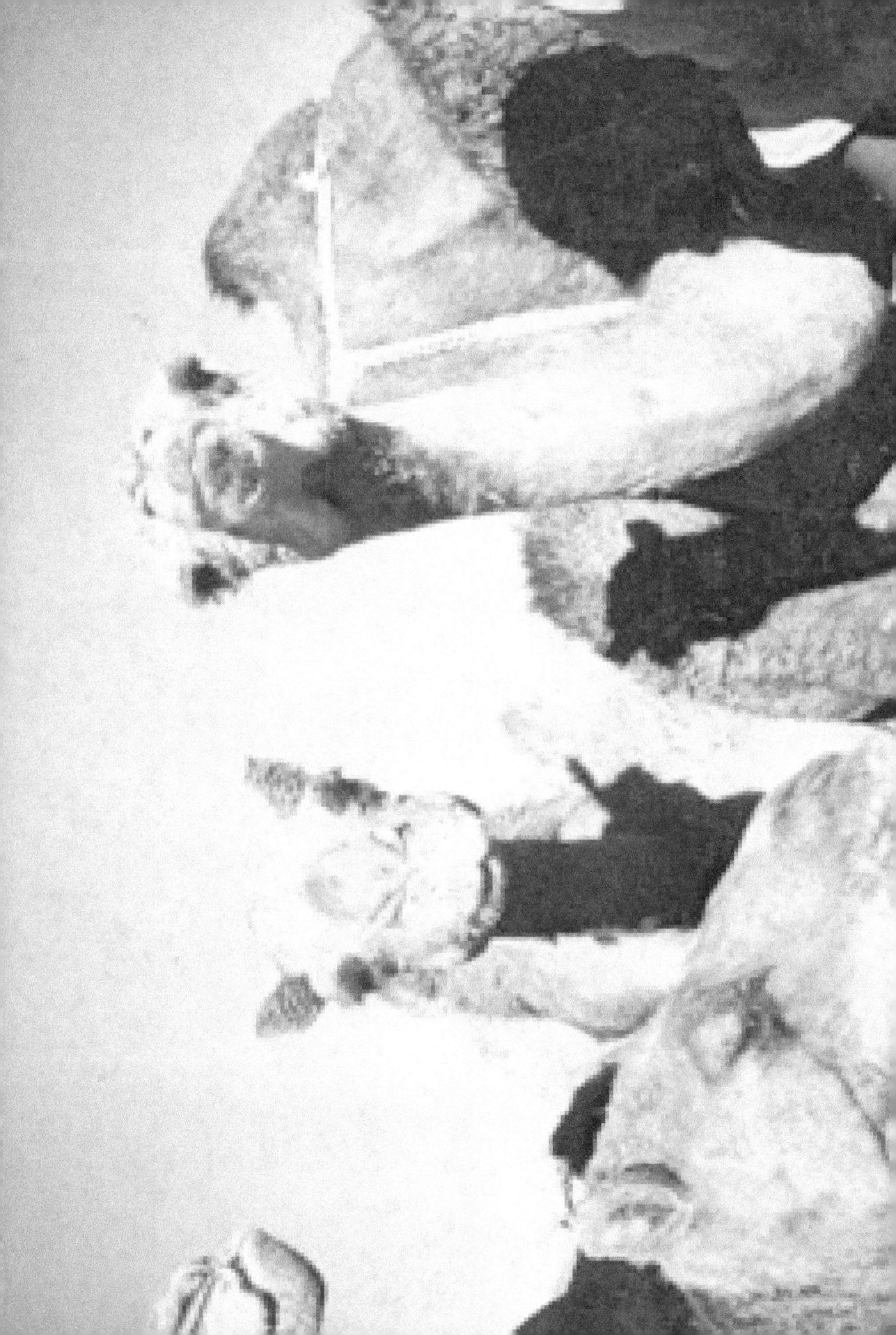

Red Flowers

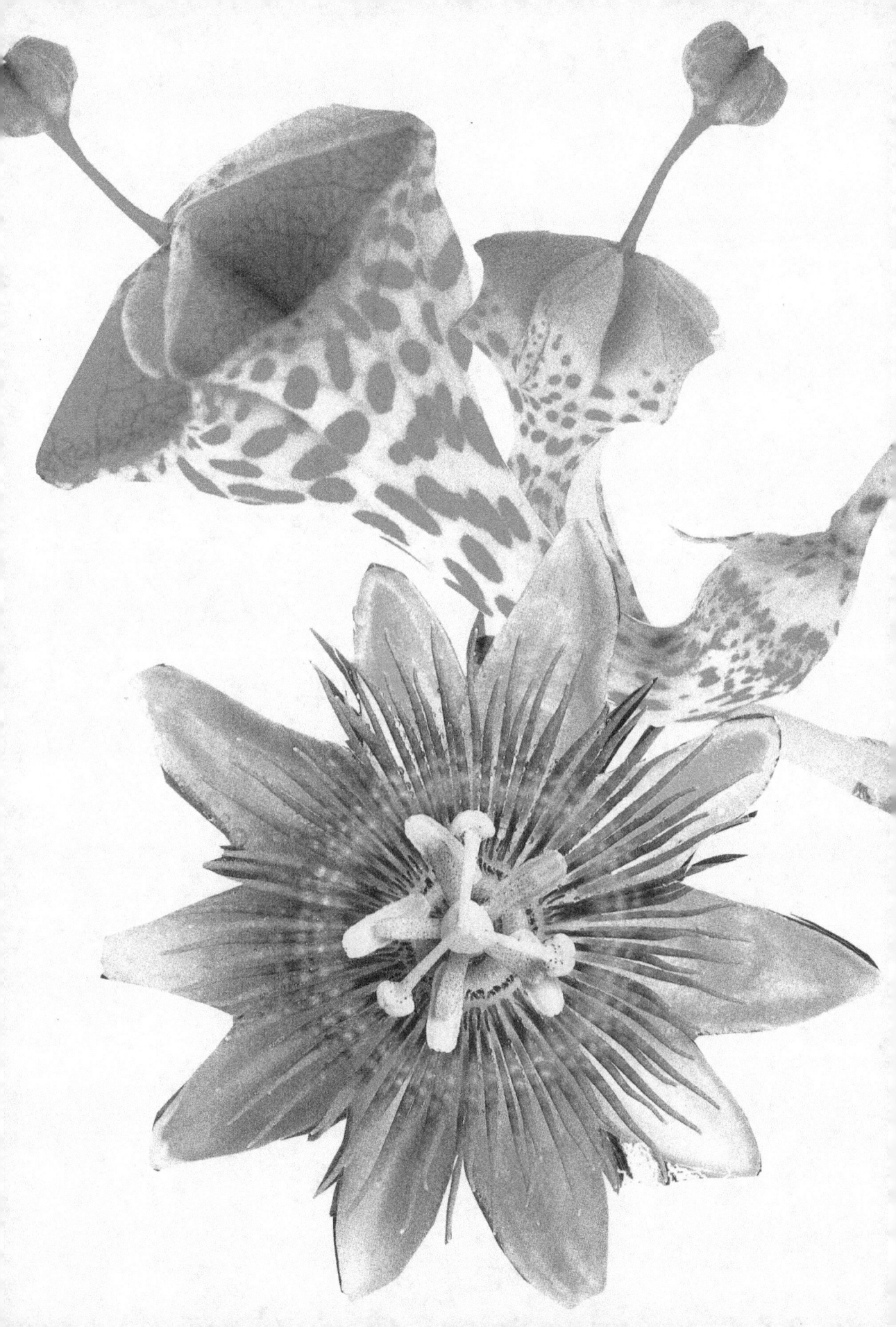

Seashells of my Mind

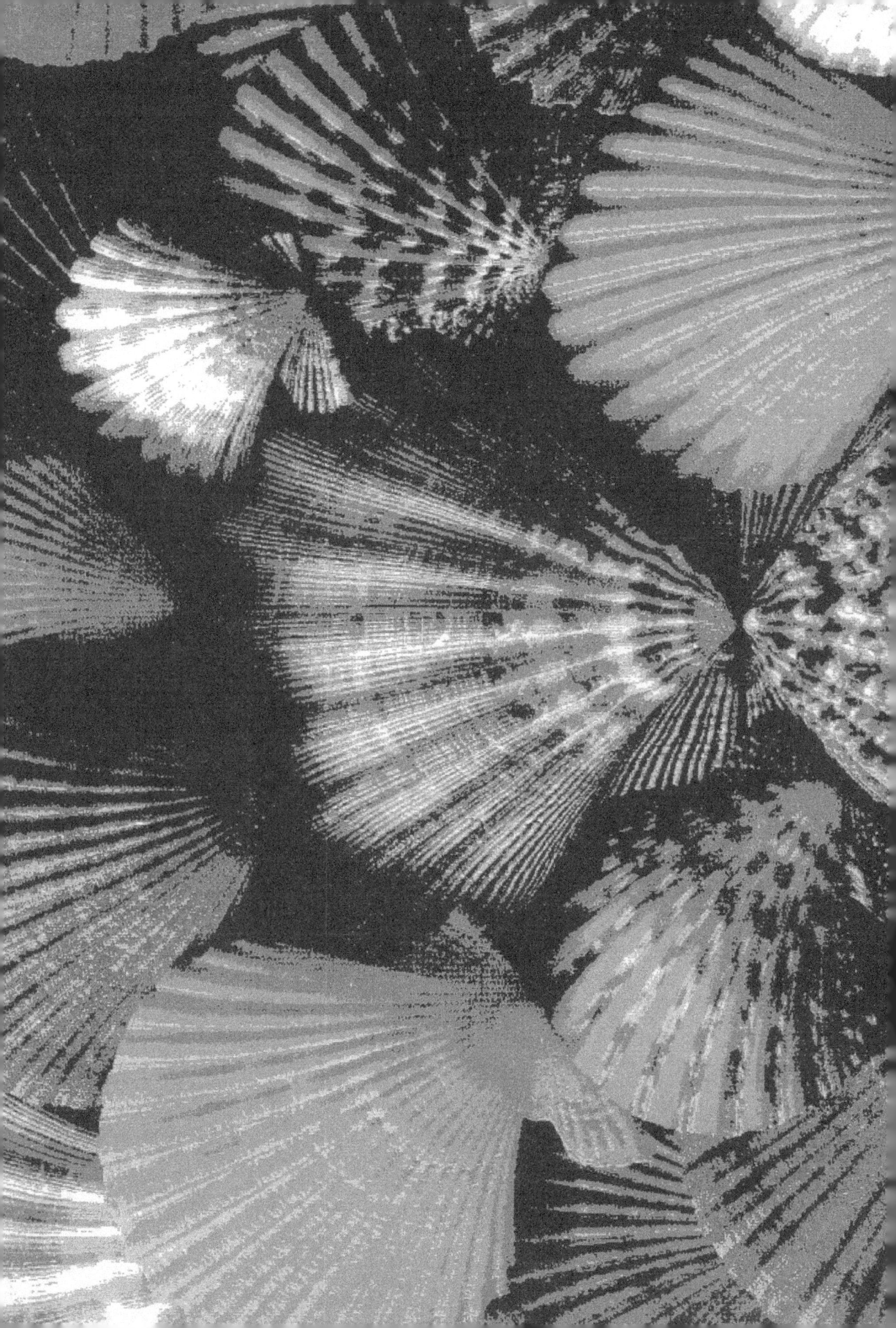

Sunflowers

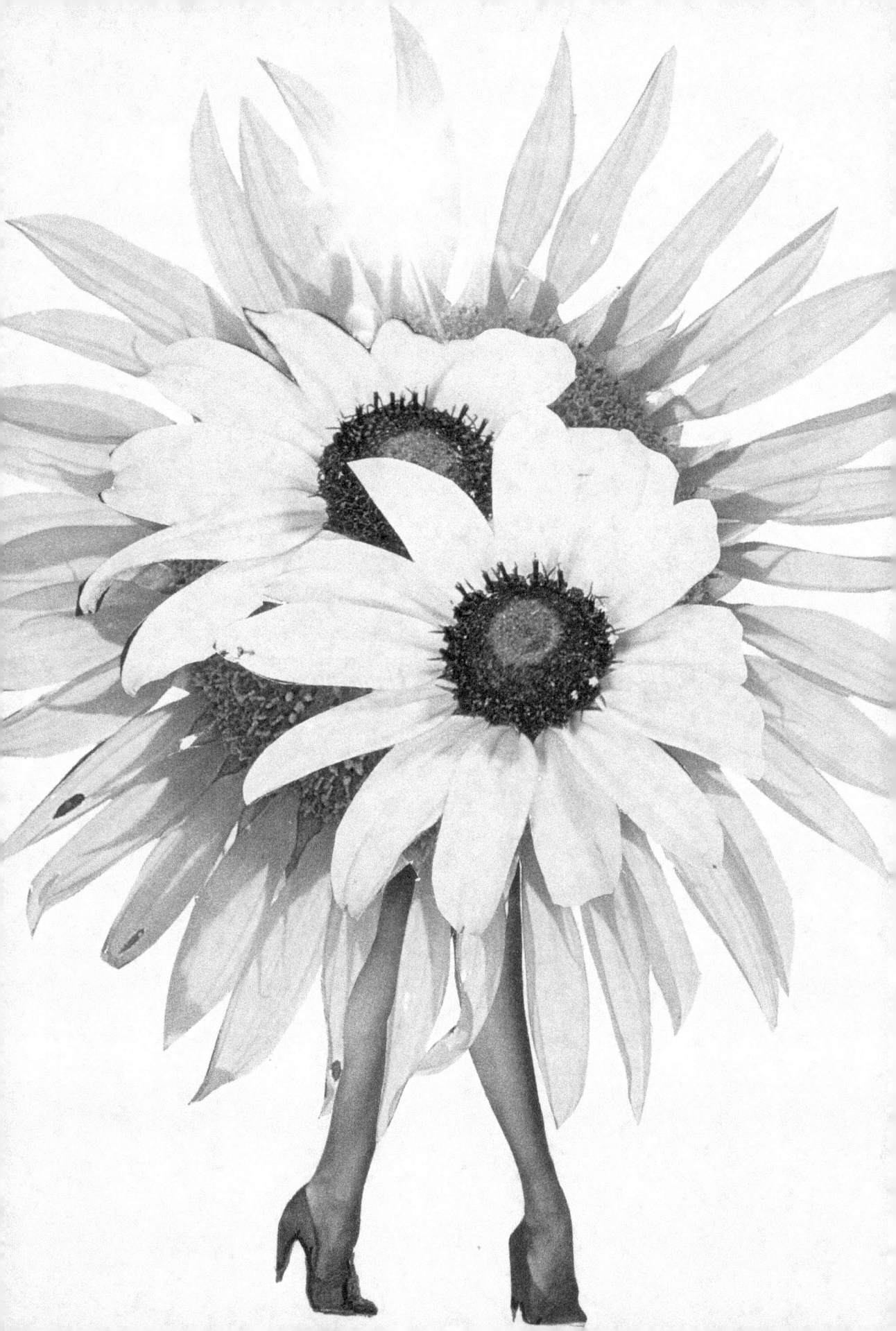

My first New York Magazine cover story

CENTS

MARCH 1, 1976

NEW YORK

Hollywood Fights Back

Moviemakers Tell You What They Really Think of the Critics
And Take Aim at:

Paul Zimmerman
Charles Champlin
Vincent Canby
Judith Crist
Andrew Sarris
Pauline Kael
Rex Reed
Gene Shalit
John Simon
Jay Cocks

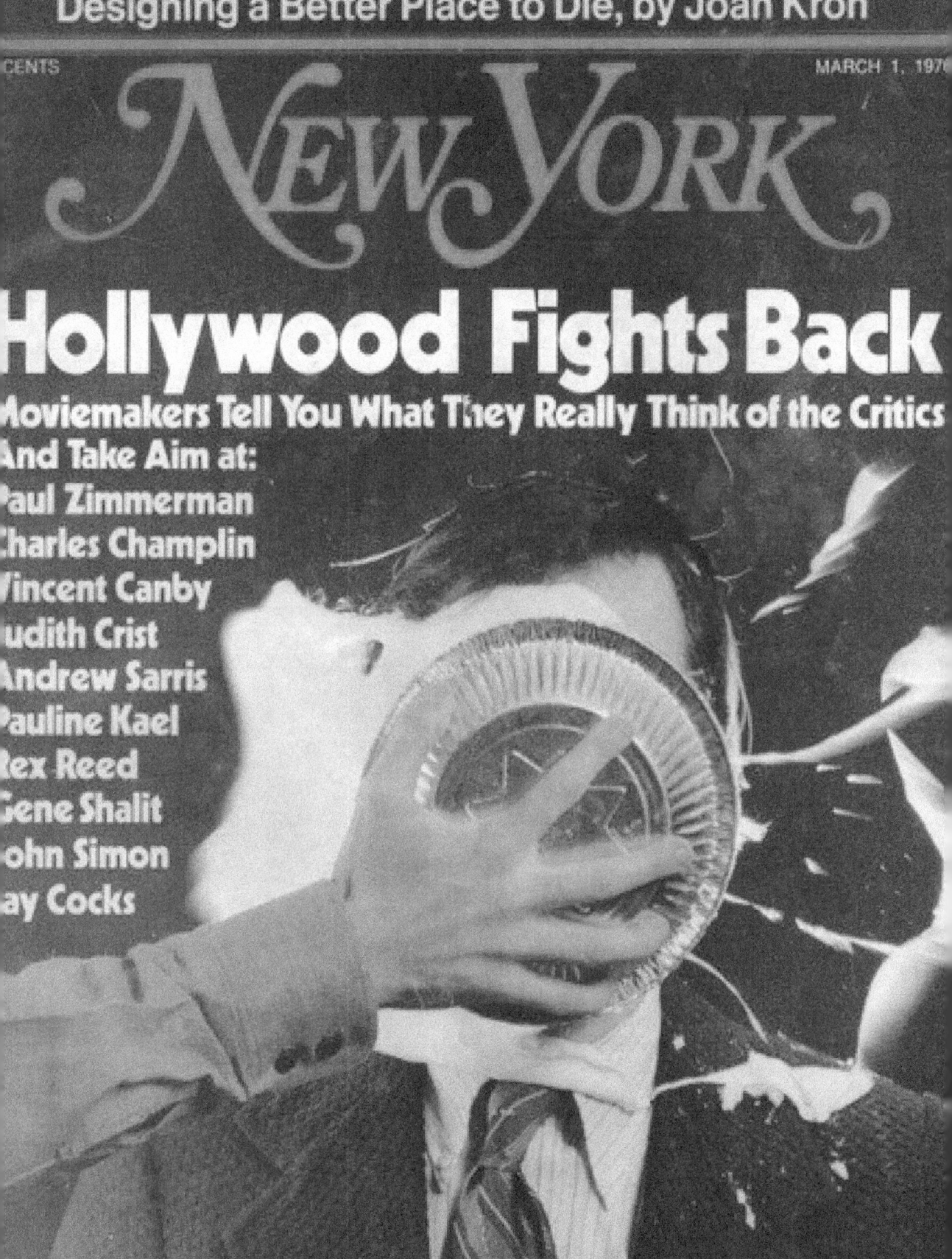

A
Hollywood
Romance

I have a particular
vulnerability to bastards.
I love ladies' men.
Men with style.

I like the dangerous. . .
a little macho
and some little boy
in a man.

Unpredictability.
Mystery.
Passion.
Him.

He is a dream that keeps
interfering with my waking life
He is the possibility
of midnight passion

He says I am his slave. I can hardly
disagree. Within finely drawn parameters,
yet beyond some earthly boundaries, I do
belong to him.

I just stare at him. For hours while he sleeps. Something wakes him. He opens his eyes and sees me staring at him. He takes me in his arms and wraps his body around mine like no one has ever done before. Possessed. Completely. Hands and feet curled under him. He falls back to sleep.

He does the most awful things
to me, and I love him.

He does not let go of me—my hands,
my mouth. All night, he does not
let go of me.

He puts me in the most embarrassing
and humiliating positions, and I
accept it. I enjoy it in some strange
way because he forces me to let go.
He takes me from behind and
doesn't stop or hold still when
I beg and the pain seems unbearable.
I love him for showing no mercy.

Jealousy is not one of the games
we play. Slave, lover, child, queen—
we play those all the time.

Sometimes he does show mercy.
But only after hurting me a
little more. You must come
one more time, and then you
can drink something. I'll leave
it in for a few more minutes,
then you can get up.

He made me put him inside of me,
then he pinned my hands tight against the pillow.
Only when he fell asleep hours Later
were my wrists once again free.

I pray for him to come.
When it is morning,
there is a small sadness
at another night without him.

I never know when he will
come, where I will see
him, when he will want
me. But I know, in spite
of myself, I will want him.
Even when I hate him, I
will still want him.

He hit me because I laughed at him.
He lectured me about my proper role.
He said we both needed for it to be this way.
Then he held me like a child
and then made love to me
until I cried and laughed.

He explains that he
must always be the king
and I will always be the slave.
But it is
a highly desirable position for me
because he will always make love to me
as if I am a Queen and he is a slave.
Queen or slave,
they are only labels.
I am complete with him;
I am rich with him.

He always talks
when he's inside of me.
He says wild, crazy,
Brilliant things.
He makes me confess to the most awful vulnerability.
Give it to me.
I hear it spoken in everyday conversation,
and my skin crawls,
my knees get liquid and warm,
and so do I.

The dog wakes me from deep sleep.
The sun rises as he opens the door.
The commands begin. Take it off.
Put it in. In the bathroom, where
he finds me brushing my teeth
furiously.
Four in the morning.
Asleep for hours.
No conversation.
Over the tub.
On my knees.
Suck it. Take all of it.
Thank God I carpeted the bathroom, I think.
Thank God he came back,
I think even more.

The way he kisses me
why?

Very often,
he reminds me
that I am his slave forever.
It is a lifetime condition
an agreement that cannot be broken.
I love it when he says this.
It makes me feel secure
that I have a destiny.

Tonight I am sure he will come.
When I awake, it is morning alone
and the usual small sadness at
another night without him.

At some outrageous hour,
He awakens me from an unwanted sleep.
He reaches me
before I get to the top of the stairs,
pushing me to my knees.

He tells me that even when
we both have grandchildren,
I will still be his slave.
He asks me, aren't I glad?
Isn't that a wonderful thing
to grow old knowing?

He comes early and stays late.
Takes me gently
and then makes me cry.
Holds me like a waif.
He offers to keep me
if I promise to have no other men.
I consider.
Under his thumb.
I do not answer.
He does not return for many months.

I want him
but don't know how to find him.
I don't even know how he spells his name.
I simply must wait.

He doesn't come for three months.
I pray to see him.
Finally, he arrives.
He slaps my face.
"Don't stay away so long next time,"
he tells me.

He always arrives in the middle of the night.
I wake up fuzzy,
and he finds me irresistible.
He tells me I'm beautiful
when the truth is his chic,
delicious,
dangerous,
outrageous beauty overwhelms me.
I rush to the bathroom to brush my Teeth
before disappearing into him.

He tells me what he likes
for breakfast
and not to talk
in the morning.
Like a ritual
I must submit
Not just in word but in deed.

It is hard to fall asleep at night. I
always want to see him. One—
thirty, fitful sleep when he
Doesn't come. He's still at the discos, two—thirty
he's just leaving, four-thirty—he's not
coming again. I want not to
want him, to wake up one
morning and not wish he was
here, not be sorry he didn't come
again.

He always smells delicious
of soap and rum and French cologne.
After he leaves
I return to bed
to savor
the warm fragrance of his sleep.

He likes to pin my hands
and feet above my head.
After a while, they hurt.
I beg him to let me down.
You know we both like it
like this. I trick him to
get free. He grabs my hair and
turns me over.
"You forget you are a slave."
His hand comes down again and
again. When I'm screaming in pain
he stops the game
and makes me look
at him. "The next time you
forget you're a slave, I'm
going to spank you like a
little girl. You understand?
Like a little girl."

He comes back, and once again,
I lose myself in between pleasure
and sweet pain.

I am liberated, unencumbered, and free.
Yet I am one hundred percent his slave.
He makes me beg for mercy
and then shows me none.
He knows just how much I can Take
and not how much I want to take.
He always pushes it to the limit.

Finally, he says he loves me.
Tears of relief. The release
of crying. He makes me
suck his cock.
He laughs.
See,
you can't cry
with your mouth full.

Tonight he talks nonsense.
Just before the sun rises
and we drift off,
I drift into sleep, smiling.
I am complete with him.
If shackled, it is willing,
for I am the happiest of slaves
with him.

The insistent early morning knocking
awakens me to insecurity.
He's too proud to tell me he loves me,
and I'm too proud to love him if he won't.

My life would be so much emptier
without him.
Yet my growing outrage
sends him away
at the slightest
encouragement. I do not like
the high price of self-respect.

His arrogance is unbearable.
I want my freedom on a night
when he wants me.
In a moment of passion,
I attempt to end it.
He tells me to be careful,
that the sacrifice will soon pay off
and then he makes love to me
for four and a half hours.

All my plans to end it
disappear
when he smiles.
Half white, half black,
a famous artist
educated in Hollywood,
Harvard,
and the world.
Physically,
He is the most beautiful man
in my life.
An outrageous face.
The grace and stealth of a panther.
The smile of a child.

I find it humorous
when he tries to be romantic.
In a reckless moment
he pledges his undying love to me.
I laugh.
He slaps me,
and I cry.
Not so much from the pain
but from the shock.
He kisses away my tears
reminding me
that we both need it to be this way.
He holds me like a child
and makes love to me until I have the hiccups
from laughing.

He calls again.
This time I take a taxi.
Thirty miles.
His new house.
He pays the cab driver
and tips him ten dollars.
Then we make love in his bed.
He tells me he loves me.
That he's always loved me.

He is sometimes too charming
to be true.
Completely unattainable.
The most tragic love.

He comes back only six days later and
is very tender. Gentle. Luxurious and
perfectly comfortable. I relax, listening
to his faintly humorous patter.
You see
Now I hold you like an equal.
And it feels good. Yes? It feels
very good to me also. But you relax.
If I held you for very long,
we'd both go to sleep.
That's why
I must be the master,
and you must be the slave.
I don't want our time to get her to be spent sleeping.
Now, suck my cock.

My name is on the front page
of the newspaper
He pretends to have already seen it
and throws it in the fire
He pushes me to my knees.
You are only a slave
he reminds me.

Sometimes
often
I want to have the strength
to send him away,
to not go looking for him,
to give him up
and never feel his touch again.
If I ever get that strong,
it will be an older, colder world.

You are the best part,
I don't want you hurt.
Before I didn't care.
Now it is different.

Though the truth of our passion defies
most moral standards, with him, there is
a quality of honesty that is absent
everywhere else in my life.

I sent him away
three times in a row.
I will not cry again.
Unless he doesn't come back . .

And he finally returns again.
This time, he wants to talk,
to question our meaning
and that of the universe.
How far can you take it?
Where?
In your heart.
I have no heart.
I know.
Don't be glib . . .
how far?
Take what?
You know.
I don't know.
If it can't be defined,
how can it have any pre-determined boundaries?
While it is alive, it will grow.
When it dies, it will decay.
It is simply life.

We talk about freedom.
He says it is only a word.

My life changes,
and his midnight visits
become tiresome.
I decide I'm no longer his slave.
He treats me badly
and I want it better.

And still,
I wait on him like a slave
long after the absences
have caused my heart to harden.
Remembering past ecstasy,
I dig deep into my soul
only to find nonexistent vulnerability.
I try to hide that truth
knowing he sees everything.

He arrives
smelling wonderful
but I am determined to send him away.
He laughs and takes off his clothes
charming,
wanting me to forgive.
This time, I can't.
It's really over. Enough.
I've changed. He hasn't.
I no longer feel secure
simply because
someday he will come back.
He listens to everything but my words.
A slave has no rights, he says,
and he gets into my bed.

Long after I am sure
he will never return,
I see him in a restaurant.
We greet as old friends
until he catches my eyes
and sees into my heart.
He buttons up my low-cut shirt
as if to tell me
I will always belong to him.

I call him a whore.
I tell him I hate him.
He smiles calmly and takes me in his arms.
I have no choice.
I belong to him.

The day comes when I refuse to obey
his commands,
which he accepts
with infuriating nonchalance.
For many years, you have been my slave,
but now I set you free.
I want my daughter to be like you
when she grows up.

Growth makes truth
invade our magic world.
It hurts to hold him.
Sorry isn't enough.

I call him a whore. I tell him
I hate him. He smiles calmly
and takes me in his arms. I
have no choice. I belong to him.

The day comes when I refuse to obey his commands, which he accepts with infuriating nonchalance. "For many years, you have been my slave, but now I set you free. I want my daughter to be like you when she grows up."

Growth makes truth invade our magic
world. I hurt to hold him. Sorry isn't
enough.

And then after what seemed like forever, he just never came back.

THE END

www.ingramcontent.com/pod-product-compliance
Lightning Source LLC
Chambersburg PA
CBHW081718220526
45468CB00008B/1893